# cakes
## ...made simple

First published in 2012
LOVE FOOD is an imprint of Parragon Books Ltd

Parragon
Queen Street House
4 Queen Street
Bath BA1 1HE, UK

www.parragon.com

ISBN: 978-1-4454-6795-5

Printed in China

Produced by Ivy Contract
Cover design by Talking Design

### Picture acknowledgements

The publisher would like to thank the following for permission to reproduce copyright material on the cover:
Chocolate Cake © Gentl & Hyers/Getty Images

### Notes for the Reader

This book uses imperial, metric, and US cup measurements. Follow the same units of measurement throughout;
do not mix imperial and metric. All spoon measurements are level: teaspoons are assumed to be 5 ml, and
tablespoons are assumed to be 15 ml. Unless otherwise stated, milk is assumed to be whole and eggs are medium.

The times given are an approximate guide only. Preparation times differ according to the techniques used by
different people and the cooking times may also vary from those given as a result of the different oven used.
Optional ingredients, variations, or serving suggestions have not been included in the calculations.

Recipes using raw or very lightly cooked eggs should be avoided by infants, the elderly, pregnant women,
convalescents, and anyone with a chronic condition. Pregnant and breast-feeding women are advised to avoid
eating peanuts and peanut products. People with nut allergies should be aware that some of the prepared
ingredients used in the recipes in this book may contain nuts. Always check the package before use.

# cakes

# introduction

There is something about a homemade cake that is truly joyous. The love and care conveyed in bakin
treats for friends and loved ones; the nostalgic memories of childhood favorites brought to life; th
satisfaction of mixing together a bowlful of unpromising ingredients, only for it to be transformed into
heavenly creation. The sheer variety of styles and flavors you can use in cake baking means you can creat
something delightful for every taste, from chocoholic to fruit fanatic.

Not only is cake baking so satisfying, it is also incredibly easy. None of the recipes in this book requi
specialist skills or obscure ingredients. In fact, the ease with which you can create a fabulous tasting cak
means that involving kids with the baking process can be very rewarding and great fun—and a good wa
to introduce children to the joy of cooking and creating food. The promise of a frosting covered spoon c
mixing bowl to lick will probably tempt any young cook into helping out!

Most of the recipes in this book require only a mixing bowl, wooden spoon, sifter, measuring equipment, wire rack, and a couple of cake pans. If you are planning on baking regularly, it's worth investing in cake pans of a few different shapes and sizes, including muffin pans. Both an electric food processor and electric mixer can really cut down the time and effort involved in getting cake mixes and toppings smooth and fluffy. Once you have mastered the basics of cake baking, the beauty is you can add your own creative flair to the recipes included here—add some chopped nuts to your muffin mix or replace water with lemon juice in your frosting, and the recipes listed here can multiply into endless scrumptious variations. From recipes for decadent chocolate gâteaux and fruity tray bakes, to elegant macaroons, you will find inspiration on the following pages to create a great cake to suit any occasion. And after making and sharing a few of the following recipes, you certainly won't find yourself short of people to share them with!

# favorites

# strawberry layer cake

## ingredients

*serves 6–8*

oil or melted butter,
  for greasing
1½ cups all-purpose flour
1 tbsp baking powder
¾ cup unsalted butter,
  softened
generous ¾ cup superfine
  sugar
3 eggs, beaten
1 tsp vanilla extract
2 tbsp milk

### filling

¼ cup unsalted butter,
  softened
1 cup confectioners' sugar,
  plus extra for dusting
½ tsp vanilla extract
3 tbsp strawberry jelly

## method

**1** Preheat the oven to 350°F/180°C. Grease two 8-inch/20-cm layer cake pans and line the bottoms with parchment paper.

**2** Sift the flour and baking powder into a large bowl and add the butter, superfine sugar, eggs, and vanilla extract. Beat well until the batter is smooth, then stir in the milk.

**3** Divide the batter between the prepared pans and smooth level. Bake in the preheated oven for 25–30 minutes, or until risen, firm, and golden brown. Let cool in the pans for 2–3 minutes, then turn out onto a wire rack to finish cooling.

**4** For the filling, beat together the butter, confectioners' sugar, and vanilla extract until smooth. Spread this mixture on top of one of the cakes. Spread the bottom of the other cake with the jelly and then sandwich the two cakes together to enclose the filling, pressing down lightly. Dust the cake with confectioners' sugar before serving.

# chocolate fudge cake

## ingredients

### serves 8

oil or melted butter,
   for greasing
2 oz/55 g semisweet
   chocolate, broken into
   pieces
2 tbsp milk
1½ cups all-purpose flour
1 tbsp baking powder
¾ cup unsalted butter,
   softened
generous ¾ cup dark
   brown sugar
3 eggs, beaten
1 tsp vanilla extract
grated chocolate, to decorate

### filling & frosting

3½ oz/100 g semisweet
   chocolate, broken into pieces
4 tbsp unsalted butter,
   softened
1½ cups confectioners' sugar
1 tsp vanilla extract
1 tbsp milk

## method

*1* Preheat the oven to 350°F/180°C. Grease a 9-inch/
   23-cm round cake pan and line with parchment paper.

*2* Put the chocolate and milk into a small saucepan and
   heat gently until melted. Remove from the heat.

*3* Sift the flour and baking powder into a large bowl
   and add the butter, brown sugar, eggs, and vanilla
   extract. Beat well until smooth, then stir in the melted
   chocolate mixture, mixing evenly. Spoon the batter
   into the prepared pan and smooth level. Bake in the
   preheated oven for 50–60 minutes, or until firm to the
   touch and just beginning to shrink away from the sides
   of the pan.

*4* Let cool in the pan for 10 minutes, then turn out onto
   wire racks to finish cooling. When cold, carefully slice
   the cake horizontally into 2 layers.

*5* For the filling and frosting, melt the chocolate with the
   butter in a small pan over low heat. Remove from the
   heat and stir in the confectioners' sugar, vanilla extract,
   and milk, then beat well until smooth.

*6* Sandwich the cake layers together with half the
   chocolate mixture, then spread the remainder on top
   of the cake, swirling with a spatula. Sprinkle with the
   grated chocolate before serving.

# grasshopper cake

## ingredients

*serves 8*

generous 1 cup milk
1 tbsp lemon juice
2½ cups self-rising flour
2 tbsp unsweetened cocoa
1 tsp baking soda
scant ½ cup butter, softened,
    plus extra for greasing
generous 1 cup superfine sugar
2 extra large eggs
3½ oz/100 g semisweet chocolate,
    melted
1 oz/25 g milk chocolate shavings,
    to decorate

### frosting

scant 1 cup unsalted butter,
    softened
generous 1 cup heavy cream
3½ cups confectioners' sugar, sifted
1 tsp peppermint extract
few drops of green food coloring

## method

1 Preheat the oven to 325°F/160°C. Grease and line an 8-inch/20-cm round deep cake pan.

2 Pour the milk into a pitcher and add the lemon juice. Let stand for 15 minutes. Sift the flour, cocoa, and baking soda into a large bowl. Add the butter, superfine sugar, and eggs and pour in the milk mixture. Beat with an electric handheld mixer until thoroughly combined. Whisk in the melted chocolate.

3 Spoon the batter into the prepared pan and smooth the surface. Bake in the preheated oven for about 1¼ hours, or until the cake is risen and a toothpick inserted into the center comes out clean. Cool in the pan, then turn out onto a wire rack to cool completely.

4 For the frosting, place the butter in a bowl and beat with an electric mixer until pale and creamy. Beat in two-thirds of the cream, then gradually beat in the confectioners' sugar. Add the rest of the cream and continue beating for 1–2 minutes, until the buttercream is very light and fluffy. Stir in the peppermint extract and food coloring to create a pale green color.

5 Slice the cake horizontally into three equal rounds. Sandwich the rounds together with half the buttercream Spread the remaining buttercream over the cake. Decorate with the chocolate shavings. Slice and serve.

# angel food cake

## ingredients

*serves 10*

oil or melted butter,
    for greasing
1 cup all-purpose flour, plus
    extra for dusting
8 extra large egg whites
1 tsp cream of tartar
1 tsp almond extract
1¼ cups superfine sugar

## topping

2¼ cups berries, such as
    strawberries and raspberries
1 tbsp lemon juice
2 tbsp confectioners' sugar

## method

*1* Preheat the oven to 325°F/160°C. Brush the inside of a 7½-cup angel cake pan with oil and dust lightly with flour.

*2* In a large grease-free bowl, whisk the egg whites until they hold soft peaks. Add the cream of tartar and whisk again until the whites are stiff but not dry.

*3* Whisk in the almond extract, then add the sugar a tablespoon at a time, whisking hard between each addition. Sift in the flour and fold in lightly and evenly using a large metal spoon.

*4* Spoon the batter into the prepared cake pan and tap on the counter to remove any large air bubbles. Bake in the preheated oven for 40–45 minutes, or until golden brown and firm to the touch.

*5* Run the tip of a small knife around the edge of the cake to loosen from the pan. Let cool in the pan for 10 minutes, then turn out the cake onto a wire rack to finish cooling.

*6* For the topping, place the berries, lemon juice, and confectioners' sugar in a saucepan and heat gently until the sugar has dissolved. Spoon on top of the cake. Slice and serve.

# boston cream pie

## ingredients

*serves 10*

4 extra large eggs
generous ½ cup superfine sugar
1 cup all-purpose flour
3 tbsp butter, melted and cooled,
    plus extra for greasing

### filling

2 eggs
¼ cup superfine sugar
1 tsp vanilla extract
2 tbsp all-purpose flour
2 tbsp cornstarch
1¼ cups milk
⅔ cup heavy cream,
    softly whipped

### topping

4 oz/115 g semisweet
    chocolate, grated
1 tbsp light corn syrup
2 tbsp unsalted butter
⅔ cup heavy cream

## method

1 Preheat the oven to 350°F/180°C. Grease and line two 9-inch/23-cm round layer cake pans.

2 Place the eggs and sugar in a heatproof bowl set over a saucepan of simmering water. Using an electric mixer beat together until the mixture is thick and pale. Sift in the flour and fold in gently. Pour the butter in a thin stream over the mixture and fold in. Divide between the prepared pans and bake in the preheated oven for 20–25 minutes. Cool in the pans for 5 minutes, then turn out onto a wire rack to cool completely.

3 For the pastry cream, whisk together the eggs, sugar, and vanilla extract. Blend the flour and cornstarch to a paste with 4 tablespoons of the milk, then whisk into the egg mixture. Heat the remaining milk until almost boiling and pour onto the egg mixture, stirring continuously. Return to the pan and cook over low heat, whisking continuously, until smooth and thickened. Pour into a bowl, cool, then fold in the whipped cream. For the glaze, place the chocolate, light corn syrup, and butter in a heatproof bowl. Heat the cream, then pour it over the chocolate. Let stand, then stir until smooth.

4 To assemble, sandwich the cakes together with the pastry cream. Spread the chocolate glaze over the top of the cake. Cut into slices to serve.

# sponge roll

## ingredients

*serves 8*

oil or melted butter,
    for greasing
1⅓ cups all-purpose flour
1½ tsp baking powder
¾ cup unsalted butter, softened
generous ¾ cup superfine sugar,
    plus extra for sprinkling
3 eggs, beaten
1 tsp vanilla extract
2 tbsp milk
scant ½ cup raspberry jelly,
    warmed

## method

*1* Preheat the oven to 350°F/180°C. Grease and line a 9- x 13-inch/23- x 33-cm jelly roll pan with the paper ½ inch/1 cm above the rim. Lay a sheet of parchment paper on the counter and sprinkle with superfine sugar.

*2* Sift the flour and baking powder into a large bowl and add the butter, sugar, eggs, and vanilla extract. Beat well until the mixture is smooth, then beat in the milk.

*3* Spoon the mixture into the prepared pan and smooth into the corners with a spatula. Bake in the preheated oven for 15–20 minutes, until firm and golden brown.

*4* When baked, carefully turn out the sponge cake onto the sugared parchment paper and spread with the jelly. Roll up the sponge cake firmly from one short side to enclose the jelly, keeping the paper around the outside to hold it in place.

*5* Lift onto a wire rack to cool, removing the paper when firm. Sprinkle with superfine sugar. Cut into slices, and serve.

## variation

To add buttercream, beat together 1 cup of confectioners' sugar, 4 tablespoons of butter, and 1 tablespoon of milk and spread onto the sponge before the jam.

# carrot cake with orange frosting

## ingredients

*serves 10*

oil or melted butter,
    for greasing
1½ cups all-purpose flour
1 tbsp baking powder
1 tsp ground cinnamon
½ tsp ground ginger
¾ cup unsalted butter,
    softened
generous ¾ cup light
    brown sugar
3 eggs, beaten
2 tbsp orange juice
scant 1½ cups coarsely
    grated carrots
½ cup chopped pecans
pecan halves, to decorate

### frosting

¼ cup whole-fat cream cheese
2¼ cups confectioners' sugar
finely grated rind of 1 orange
1 tbsp orange juice, plus extra
    if needed

## method

1  Preheat the oven to 325°F/160°C. Grease and line a 9-inch/23-cm round, deep cake pan.

2  Sift the flour, baking powder, cinnamon, and ginger into a bowl and add the butter, sugar, and eggs. Beat well until smooth, then stir in the orange juice, carrots, and chopped pecans.

3  Spoon the mixture into the prepared pan and spread the top level. Bake the cake in the preheated oven for 1–1¼ hours, or until it is well risen, firm, and golden brown.

4  Let cool in the pan for 10 minutes, then turn out onto a wire rack to finish cooling.

5  For the frosting, put all the ingredients into a bowl and beat until smooth and thick, adding more orange juice if necessary. Spread over the top of the cake and decorate with pecan halves.

# coffee & walnut cake

## ingredients

*serves 8*

oil or melted butter,
    for greasing
¾ cup butter
¾ cup light brown sugar
3 extra large eggs, beaten
3 tbsp strong black coffee
1½ cups self-rising flour
1½ tsp baking powder
1 cup walnut pieces
walnut halves, to decorate

### filling & frosting

½ cup butter
1¾ cups confectioners' sugar
1 tbsp strong black coffee
½ tsp vanilla extract

## method

1 Preheat the oven to 350°F/180°C. Grease two 8-inch/
    20-cm layer cake pans and line the bottoms with
    parchment paper.

2 Cream together the butter and brown sugar until pale
    and fluffy. Gradually add the eggs, beating well after
    each addition. Beat in the coffee.

3 Sift the flour and baking powder into the batter, then
    fold in lightly and evenly with a metal spoon. Fold in
    the walnut pieces.

4 Divide the batter between the prepared cake pans
    and smooth level. Bake in the preheated oven for
    20–25 minutes, or until golden brown and springy
    to the touch. Let cool in the pans for 5 minutes, then
    turn out onto wire racks to finish cooling.

5 For the filling and frosting, beat together the butter,
    confectioners' sugar, coffee, and vanilla extract, mixing
    until smooth and creamy.

6 Use about half the mixture to sandwich the cakes
    together, then spread the remaining buttercream on
    top and swirl with a metal spatula. Decorate with
    walnut halves.

# hummingbird cake

## ingredients

*serves 10*

oil or melted butter,
    for greasing
2¼ cups all-purpose flour
1¼ cups superfine sugar
1 tsp ground cinnamon
1 tsp baking soda
3 eggs, beaten
scant 1 cup sunflower oil
scant 1 cup pecans, coarsely
    chopped, plus extra
    to decorate
1 cup mashed ripe banana
    (about 3 bananas)
3 oz/85 g canned crushed
    pineapple (drained weight),
    plus 4 tbsp juice from the can

### filling & frosting

¾ cup cream cheese
4 tbsp unsalted butter
1 tsp vanilla extract
3½ cups confectioners' sugar

## method

*1* Preheat the oven to 350°F/180°C. Grease three 9-inch/23-cm layer cake pans and line the bottoms with parchment paper.

*2* Sift together the flour, superfine sugar, cinnamon, and baking soda into a large bowl. Add the eggs, oil, pecans, bananas, pineapple, and pineapple juice and stir with a wooden spoon until evenly mixed.

*3* Divide the batter among the prepared pans and smooth level. Bake in the preheated oven for 25–30 minutes, or until golden brown and firm to the touch.

*4* Remove the cakes from the oven and let cool in the pans for 10 minutes, then turn out onto wire racks to finish cooling.

*5* For the filling and frosting, beat together the cream cheese, butter, and vanilla extract in a bowl until smooth. Sift in the confectioners' sugar and mix until smooth.

*6* Sandwich the cakes together with half of the mixture, spread the remaining frosting over the top, then sprinkle with pecans to decorate.

# lemon drizzle cake

## ingredients

*serves 8*

oil or melted butter,
    for greasing
1¾ cups all-purpose flour
2 tsp baking powder
1 cup superfine sugar
4 eggs
⅔ cup sour cream
grated rind of 1 large lemon
4 tbsp lemon juice
⅔ cup sunflower oil

### syrup

¼ cup confectioners' sugar
3 tbsp lemon juice

## method

*1* Preheat the oven to 350°F/180°C. Grease an 8-inch/20-cm loose-bottom round cake pan and line the bottom with parchment paper.

*2* Sift the flour and baking powder into a mixing bowl and stir in the superfine sugar. In a separate bowl, whisk the eggs, sour cream, lemon rind, lemon juice, and oil together. Pour the egg mixture into the dry ingredients and mix well until evenly combined.

*3* Pour the batter into the prepared pan and bake in the preheated oven for 45–60 minutes, or until risen and golden brown.

*4* For the syrup, mix together the confectioners' sugar and lemon juice in a small pan. Stir over low heat until just beginning to bubble and turn syrupy.

*5* As soon as the cake comes out of the oven, prick the surface with a fine skewer, then brush the syrup over the top. Let the cake cool completely in the pan before turning out and serving.

# pound cake

## ingredients

*serves 8–10*

¾ cup unsalted butter,
    plus extra for greasing
scant 1 cup superfine sugar
finely grated rind of 1 lemon
3 extra-large eggs, beaten
1 cup all-purpose flour
1 cup self-rising flour
2–3 tbsp brandy or milk
2 slices of citron peel

## method

*1* Preheat the oven to 325°F/160°C. Grease and line a 7-inch/18-cm round deep cake pan.

*2* Cream together the butter and sugar until pale and fluffy. Add the lemon rind and gradually beat in the eggs. Sift in the flours and fold in evenly, adding enough brandy to make a soft consistency.

*3* Spoon the batter into the prepared pan and smooth the surface. Lay the slices of citron peel on top of the cake.

*4* Bake in the preheated oven for 1–1¼ hours, or until well risen, golden brown, and springy to the touch.

*5* Cool in the pan for 10 minutes, then turn out and cool completely on a wire rack.

## variation

To make a lemon poppyseed cake, add half the juice of the lemon and 1–2 tablespoons of poppyseeds before sifting in the flours.

# gingerbread

## ingredients

*serves 9*

¾ cup butter, plus extra
    for greasing
generous ⅔ cup dark brown sugar
¾ cup dark corn syrup
finely grated rind and juice of
    1 small orange
2 extra large eggs, beaten
2 cups self-rising flour
scant ½ cup whole wheat flour
2 tsp ground ginger
3 tbsp chopped candied ginger
    or preserved ginger, plus extra
    pieces to decorate

## method

1 Preheat the oven to 350°F/180°C. Grease a 9-inch/ 23-cm square deep cake pan and line the bottom with nonstick parchment paper.

2 Place the butter, sugar, and corn syrup in a saucepan and heat gently, stirring until melted. Remove from the heat.

3 Beat in the orange rind and juice, eggs, flours, and ground ginger, then beat thoroughly to mix evenly. Stir in the chopped candied ginger.

4 Spoon the batter into the prepared pan and bake in the preheated oven for 40–45 minutes, or until risen and firm to the touch.

5 Cool in the pan for about 10 minutes, then turn out and finish cooling on a wire rack. Cut into squares and decorate with pieces of candied ginger.

# red velvet cake

## ingredients

*serves 12*

1 cup unsalted butter,
    plus extra for greasing
4 tbsp water
$\frac{1}{2}$ cup unsweetened cocoa
3 eggs
generous 1 cup buttermilk
2 tsp vanilla extract
2 tbsp red food coloring
    (or 4 tbsp beetroot juice,
    if preferred)
2$\frac{1}{2}$ cups all-purpose flour
$\frac{1}{2}$ cup cornstarch
1$\frac{1}{2}$ tsp baking powder
scant 1$\frac{1}{2}$ cups superfine sugar

### frosting

generous 1 cup cream cheese
3 tbsp unsalted butter
3 tbsp superfine sugar
1 tsp vanilla extract

## method

1 Preheat the oven to 375°F/190°C. Grease two 9-inch/23-cm layer cake pans and line the bottoms with parchment paper.

2 Place the butter, water, and cocoa in a small saucepan and heat gently, without boiling, stirring until melted and smooth. Remove the mixture from the heat and let cool slightly.

3 Beat together the eggs, buttermilk, vanilla extract, and food coloring until frothy. Beat in the butter mixture. Sift together the flour, cornstarch, and baking powder, then stir quickly and evenly into the egg mixture with the superfine sugar.

4 Divide the batter between the prepared pans and bake in the preheated oven for 25–30 minutes, or until risen and firm to the touch. Cool in the pans for 3–4 minutes, then turn out and finish cooling on a wire rack.

5 For the frosting, beat together all the ingredients until smooth. Use about half of the frosting to sandwich the cakes together, then spread the remainder over the top, swirling with a metal spatula.

# fruit cake

## ingredients

*serves 16*

scant 2½ cups golden raisins
1⅔ cups raisins
½ cup chopped plumped
  dried apricots
½ cup chopped pitted dates
4 tbsp dark rum or brandy,
  plus extra for flavoring
  (optional)
finely grated rind and juice of
  1 orange
1 cup butter, plus extra
  for greasing
1 cup light brown sugar
4 eggs, beaten
generous ⅓ cup chopped
  candied peel
⅓ cup candied cherries,
  quartered
2 tbsp chopped candied
  ginger or preserved ginger
⅓ cup chopped blanched
  almonds
1¾ cups all-purpose flour
1 tsp apple pie spice

## method

*1* Place the golden raisins, raisins, apricots, and dates in a large bowl and stir in the rum, orange rind, and orange juice. Cover and let soak for several hours or overnight.

*2* Preheat the oven to 350°F/180°C. Grease a deep 8-inch/20-cm round cake pan and line the bottom with parchment paper.

*3* Cream together the butter and sugar until light and fluffy. Gradually beat in the eggs, beating hard after each addition. Stir in the soaked fruits, candied peel, candied cherries, candied ginger, and blanched almonds.

*4* Sift together the flour and apple pie spice, then fold lightly and evenly into the batter. Spoon into the prepared cake pan and level the surface, making a slight depression in the center with the back of the spoon. Bake in the preheated oven for 2¼–2¾ hours, or until the cake is beginning to shrink away from the sides of the pan and a toothpick inserted into the center comes out clean. Cool completely in the pan.

*5* Turn out the cake and remove the lining paper. Wrap with wax paper and foil, and store for at least 2 months before use. To add a richer flavor, prick the cake with a toothpick and spoon over a couple of tablespoons of rum or brandy, if using, before storing.

# classic cherry cake

## ingredients

*serves 6*

oil or melted butter,
    for greasing
generous 1 cup candied
    cherries, quartered
¾ cup ground almonds
1¾ cups all-purpose flour
1 tsp baking powder
scant 1 cup butter
1 cup superfine sugar
3 extra large eggs, beaten
finely grated rind and juice
    of 1 lemon
6 sugar cubes, crushed

## method

*1* Preheat the oven to 350°F/180°C. Grease an 8-inch/
20-cm round cake pan and line with parchment paper.

*2* Stir together the candied cherries, ground almonds,
and 1 tablespoon of the flour. Sift the remaining flour
into a separate bowl with the baking powder.

*3* Cream together the butter and superfine sugar
until light in color and fluffy in texture. Gradually
add the eggs, beating hard with each addition, until
evenly mixed.

*4* Add the flour mixture and fold lightly and evenly into
the creamed mixture with a metal spoon. Add the
cherry mixture and fold in evenly. Finally, fold in the
lemon rind and juice.

*5* Spoon the batter into the prepared cake pan and
sprinkle with the crushed sugar cubes. Bake in the
preheated oven for 1–1¼ hours, or until risen, golden
brown, and the cake is just beginning to shrink away
from the sides of the pan.

*6* Let cool in the pan for 15 minutes, then turn out onto
a wire rack to finish cooling.

# checkerboard sponge cake

## ingredients

*serves 6–8*

½ cup butter or margarine,
    softened, plus extra
    for greasing
generous ½ cup superfine sugar,
    plus extra for sprinkling
2 eggs, lightly beaten
1 tsp vanilla extract
1 cup self-rising flour, sifted
a few drops of pink food coloring
2–3 tbsp apricot jelly
10½ oz/300 g marzipan

## method

*1* Preheat the oven to 350°F/180°C. Grease and line a 7-inch/18-cm square shallow baking pan. Cut a strip of double parchment paper and grease it. Use this to divide the pan in half.

*2* Cream the butter and sugar in a mixing bowl until pale and fluffy. Gently beat in the eggs and vanilla extract, gradually adding in the flour. Spoon half the batter into a separate bowl and mix in a few drops of food coloring. Spoon the plain batter into one half of the prepared baking pan and the colored batter into the other half of the pan. Bake in the preheated oven for 35–40 minutes. Turn out and let cool on a wire rack.

*3* When cool, trim the edges and cut the cake portions lengthwise in half, making four equal parts. Warm the jelly in a small saucepan. Brush two sides of each cake portion with some of the jelly and stick them together to create a checkerboard effect. Knead the marzipan with a few drops of food coloring to color. Roll out the marzipan to a rectangle wide enough to wrap around the cake. Brush the outside of the cake with the remaining jelly. Place the cake on the marzipan and wrap the marzipan around it, making sure that the seam is on one corner of the cake. Trim the edges neatly. Crimp the top edges of the cake, if you like, and sprinkle with sugar.

# cupcakes, muffins & bars

# vanilla frosted cupcakes

## ingredients

*makes 12*

½ cup unsalted butter, softened
generous ½ cup superfine sugar
2 eggs, lightly beaten
¾ cup self-rising flour
1 tbsp milk
candied rose petals,
    to decorate

### frosting

¾ cup unsalted butter, softened
2 tsp vanilla extract
2 tbsp milk
scant 2⅔ cups confectioners'
    sugar, sifted

## method

*1* Preheat the oven to 350°F/180°C. Put 12 paper liners in a 12-hole muffin pan.

*2* Place the butter and sugar in a bowl and beat together until light and fluffy. Gradually beat in the eggs. Sift in the flour and fold in gently using a metal spoon. Fold in the milk.

*3* Spoon the batter into the paper liners. Bake in the preheated oven for 15–20 minutes, until golden brown and firm to the touch. Transfer to a wire rack and let cool.

*4* For the frosting, put the butter, vanilla extract, and milk in a large bowl. Using a mixer, beat the mixture until smooth. Gradually beat in the confectioners' sugar and continue beating for 2–3 minutes, until the frosting is light and creamy.

*5* Spoon the frosting into a large pastry bag fitted with a large star tip and pipe swirls of the frosting onto the top of each cupcake. Decorate each cupcake with candied rose petals.

# raspberry ripple cupcakes

## ingredients

*makes 32*

1½ cups all-purpose flour
1 tbsp baking powder
1 tbsp cornstarch
¾ cup unsalted butter, softened
generous ¾ cup superfine sugar
3 eggs, beaten
1 tsp almond extract
generous 1 cup fresh raspberries
vanilla sugar, for sprinkling

## method

*1* Preheat the oven to 375°F/190°C. Put 32 paper liners into shallow muffin pans or put double-layer liners onto cookie sheets.

*2* Sift the flour, baking powder, and cornstarch into a large bowl and add the butter, sugar, eggs, and almond extract. Beat well until the mixture is smooth. Mash the raspberries lightly with a fork, then fold into the mix.

*3* Divide the mixture among the paper liners. Bake in the preheated oven for 15–20 minutes, or until risen, firm, and golden brown. Transfer the cupcakes to a wire rack to cool.

*4* Sprinkle with vanilla sugar before serving.

# chewy oatmeal cupcakes

## ingredients

*makes 8*

3 tbsp soft margarine
3 tbsp raw brown sugar
1 tbsp dark corn syrup
$2/3$ cup rolled oats

**topping**

4 tbsp butter, softened
$1/4$ cup superfine sugar
1 large egg, lightly beaten
generous $1/3$ cup self-rising flour

## method

*1* Preheat the oven to 375°F/190°C. Line a 12-hole muffin pan with 8 paper liners or put 8 double-layer paper liners on a baking sheet.

*2* For the topping, place the margarine, raw brown sugar, and corn syrup in a small saucepan and heat gently until the margarine has melted. Stir in the oats. Set aside.

*3* Put the butter and superfine sugar in a bowl and beat together until light and fluffy. Gradually beat in the egg. Sift in the flour and, using a metal spoon, fold gently into the mixture. Spoon the mixture into the paper liners. Gently spoon the oatmeal mixture over the top.

*4* Bake the cupcakes in the preheated oven for 20 minutes, or until golden brown. Transfer to a wire rack to cool completely.

# pistachio cupcakes with tangy lime frosting

## ingredients

*makes 16*

generous ¾ cup unsalted
    pistachio nuts
½ cup butter, softened
¾ cup superfine sugar
1 cup self-rising flour
2 eggs, lightly beaten
4 tbsp Greek yogurt
1 tbsp pistachio nuts,
    chopped, to decorate

### frosting

½ cup butter, softened
2 tbsp sweetened lime juice
few drops of green food
    coloring (optional)
1¾ cups confectioners' sugar

## method

*1* Preheat the oven to 350°F/180°C. Line two 12-hole muffin pans with 16 paper liners or put 16 double-layer paper liners on a baking sheet.

*2* Put the pistachio nuts in a food processor or blender and process for a few seconds until finely ground. Add the butter, sugar, flour, eggs, and yogurt and process until evenly mixed. Spoon the batter into the paper liners.

*3* Bake the cupcakes in the preheated oven for 20–25 minutes, or until well risen and springy to the touch. Transfer to a wire rack and let cool completely.

*4* For the frosting, put the butter, lime juice, and food coloring, if using, in a bowl and beat until light and fluffy. Sift in the confectioners' sugar and beat until smooth. Swirl the frosting over each cupcake and sprinkle with the chopped pistachio nuts to decorate.

# maple pecan cupcakes

## ingredients

*makes 30*

1½ cups all-purpose flour
1 tbsp baking powder
¾ cup unsalted butter, softened
generous ½ cup light
    brown sugar
4 tbsp maple syrup
3 eggs, beaten
1 tsp vanilla extract
¼ cup finely chopped pecans

### topping

⅓ cup finely chopped pecans
2 tbsp all-purpose flour
2 tbsp light brown sugar
2 tbsp melted butter

## method

*1* Preheat the oven to 375°F/190°C. Put 30 paper liners into shallow muffin pans or put 30 double-layer liners onto cookie sheets.

*2* Sift the flour and baking powder into a large bowl and add the butter, sugar, maple syrup, eggs, and vanilla extract. Beat well until the mixture is smooth, then stir in the pecans.

*3* Divide the mixture among the paper liners. For the topping, combine the pecans, flour, sugar, and melted butter to make a crumbly mixture and spoon a little on top of each cake.

*4* Bake in the preheated oven for 15–20 minutes, or until risen, firm, and golden brown. Transfer the cupcakes to a wire rack to cool.

# honey & spice cupcakes

## ingredients

*makes 24*

²/₃ cup butter
scant ½ cup light brown sugar
scant ½ cup honey
1¾ cups self-rising flour
1 tsp ground allspice
2 eggs, beaten
22–24 whole blanched almonds

## method

*1* Preheat the oven to 350°F/180°C. Place 24 paper liners in two 12-cup shallow muffin pans.

*2* Place the butter, sugar, and honey in a large saucepan and heat gently, stirring, until the butter has melted. Remove the pan from the heat.

*3* Sift together the flour and allspice and stir into the mixture in the pan, then beat in the eggs, mixing to a smooth batter.

*4* Spoon the batter into the paper liners and place a blanched almond on top of each one. Bake in the preheated oven for 20–25 minutes, or until well risen and golden brown. Transfer to a wire rack to cool.

# rocky road cupcakes

## ingredients

*makes 12*

2 tbsp unsweetened cocoa
2 tbsp hot water
½ cup butter, softened
½ cup superfine sugar
2 eggs, lightly beaten
generous ¾ cup
    self-rising flour

### topping

¼ cup chopped mixed nuts
3½ oz/100 g milk chocolate,
    melted
2 cups mini marshmallows
¼ cup candied cherries,
    chopped

## method

1 Line a 12-hole muffin pan with 12 paper liners or put 12 double-layer paper liners on a baking sheet.

2 Blend the cocoa and hot water together and set aside. Put the butter and sugar in a bowl and beat together until light and fluffy. Gradually beat in the eggs, then beat in the blended cocoa. Sift in the flour and, using a metal spoon, fold gently into the batter. Spoon the mixture into the paper liners.

3 Bake the cupcakes in the preheated oven for 20 minutes, or until well risen and springy to the touch. Transfer to a wire rack to cool completely.

4 For the topping, stir the nuts into the melted chocolate and spread a little of the mixture over the top of the cupcakes. Lightly stir the marshmallows and cherries into the remaining chocolate mixture and pile on top of the cupcakes. Let set.

# chocolate & orange cupcakes

## ingredients

### makes 16

½ cup butter, softened
generous ½ cup superfine sugar
finely grated rind and juice
    of ½ orange
2 eggs, lightly beaten
generous ¾ cup self-rising flour
1 oz/25 g semisweet chocolate,
    grated
thin strips candied orange
    peel, to decorate

### topping

4 oz/115 g semisweet chocolate,
    broken into pieces
2 tbsp unsalted butter
1 tbsp dark corn syrup

## method

1 Preheat the oven to 350°F/180°C. Line muffin pans with 16 paper liners or put 16 double-layer paper liners on a baking sheet.

2 Put the butter, sugar, and orange rind in a bowl and beat together until light and fluffy. Gradually beat in the eggs. Sift in the flour and, using a metal spoon, fold gently into the mixture with the orange juice and grated chocolate. Spoon the cake batter into the paper liners.

3 Bake in the preheated oven for 20 minutes, or until well risen and springy to the touch. Transfer to a wire rack and let cool.

4 For the frosting, put the chocolate into a heatproof bowl and add the butter and syrup. Set the bowl over a saucepan of simmering water and heat until melted. Remove from the heat and stir until smooth. Cool until the frosting is thick enough to spread. Spread over the cupcakes and decorate each cupcake with a few strips of candied orange peel. Let set.

# coffee fudge cupcakes

## ingredients

### *makes 28*

1½ cups all-purpose flour
1 tbsp baking powder
¾ cup unsalted butter, softened
generous ¾ cup superfine sugar
3 eggs, beaten
1 tsp coffee extract
2 tbsp milk
chocolate-covered coffee beans,
    to decorate

### frosting

¼ cup unsalted butter
generous ½ cup light brown
    sugar
2 tbsp light cream or milk
½ tsp coffee extract
3½ cups confectioners' sugar,
    sifted

## method

1 Preheat the oven to 375°F/190°C. Put 28 paper liners into shallow muffin pans or put 28 double-layer liners onto baking sheets.

2 Sift the flour and baking powder into a large bowl and add the butter, superfine sugar, eggs, and coffee extract. Beat well until the mixture is smooth, then beat in the milk.

3 Divide the mixture among the paper liners. Bake in the preheated oven for 15–20 minutes, or until risen, firm, and golden brown. Transfer the cupcakes to a wire rack to cool.

4 For the frosting, put the butter, brown sugar, cream, and coffee extract into a pan over medium heat and stir until smooth. Bring to a boil and boil for 2 minutes, stirring. Remove from the heat and beat in the confectioners' sugar.

5 Stir until smooth and thick, then spoon into a pastry bag fitted with a large star tip. Pipe a swirl of frosting on top of each cupcake and top with a coffee bean.

# butterscotch cupcakes

## ingredients

*makes 28*

1½ cups all-purpose flour
1 tbsp baking powder
¾ cup unsalted butter, softened
generous ¾ cup light brown
    sugar
3 eggs, beaten
1 tsp vanilla extract

### topping

2 tbsp dark corn syrup
2 tbsp unsalted butter
2 tbsp dark brown sugar

## method

1 Preheat the oven to 375°F/190°C. Put 28 paper liners into shallow muffin pans or put 28 double-layer liners onto baking sheets.

2 Sift the flour and baking powder into a large bowl and add the butter, sugar, eggs, and vanilla extract. Beat well until the mixture is smooth.

3 Divide the mixture among the paper liners. Bake in the preheated oven for 15–20 minutes, or until risen, firm, and golden brown. Transfer the cupcakes to a wire rack to cool.

4 For the topping, put the corn syrup, butter, and sugar into a small pan and heat gently, stirring, until the sugar dissolves. Bring to a boil and cook, stirring, for about 1 minute. Drizzle the mixture over the cupcakes and let set.

# blueberry & vanilla muffins

## ingredients

### makes 18

1 cup self-rising flour
½ tsp baking powder
generous ½ cup superfine sugar
generous ½ cup blueberries
2 tsp vanilla extract
1 egg
½ cup buttermilk
2 tbsp vegetable oil
vanilla sugar, for dusting

## method

*1* Preheat the oven to 375°F/190°C. Cut out 18 x 3½-inch 9-cm squares from parchment paper. Push the squares into 2 x 12-hole mini muffin pans, creasing the squares to fit so that they form paper liners. Don't worry if they lift out of the sections slightly; the weight of the muffin batter will hold them in place.

*2* Sift the flour and baking powder into a mixing bowl. Stir in the sugar and blueberries. In a separate mixing bowl, beat together the vanilla, egg, buttermilk, and oil with a fork until evenly combined.

*3* Turn the buttermilk mixture into the flour. Using a metal spoon, gently fold the ingredients together until only just mixed. Don't overblend the ingredients or the muffins won't be as light.

*4* Spoon the batter into the paper liners; it should be level with the top of the pan. Sprinkle with a little vanilla sugar and bake in the preheated oven for 15 minutes, or until risen and just firm to the touch. Let the muffins stand in the pan for 2 minutes, then transfer them in their liners to a wire rack to cool. Serve warm or cold, dusted with extra vanilla sugar.

# double chocolate brownies

## ingredients

### makes 9

1/2 cup butter, plus extra
    for greasing
4 oz/115 g semisweet chocolate,
    broken into pieces
1 1/3 cups superfine sugar
pinch of salt
1 tsp vanilla extract
2 eggs
1 cup all-purpose flour
2 tbsp unsweetened cocoa
1/2 cup white chocolate chips

### sauce

4 tbsp butter
generous 1 cup superfine sugar
2/3 cup milk
generous 1 cup heavy cream
2/3 cup dark corn syrup
7 oz/200 g semisweet chocolate,
    broken into pieces

## method

**1** Preheat the oven to 350°F/180°C. Grease a 7-inch/
18-cm square cake pan and line the bottom with
parchment paper.

**2** Place the butter and chocolate in a small heatproof
bowl set over a saucepan of gently simmering water
until melted. Stir until smooth. Let cool slightly. Stir in
the sugar, salt, and vanilla extract. Add the eggs, one
at a time, stirring well, until blended.

**3** Sift the flour and cocoa into the cake batter and beat
until smooth. Stir in the chocolate chips, then pour
the batter into the prepared pan. Bake in the preheated
oven for 35–40 minutes, or until the top is evenly
colored and a toothpick inserted into the center
comes out almost clean. Let cool slightly while you
prepare the sauce.

**4** For the sauce, place the butter, sugar, milk, cream,
and corn syrup in a small saucepan and heat gently
until the sugar has dissolved. Bring to a boil and stir
for 10 minutes, or until the mixture is caramel-colored.
Remove from the heat and add the chocolate. Stir until
smooth. Cut the brownies into squares and serve
immediately with the sauce.

# vanilla swirled brownies

## ingredients

*makes 12*

6 tbsp lightly salted butter,
 plus extra for greasing
3½ oz/100 g semisweet
 chocolate, coarsely chopped
1 egg
1 egg yolk
½ cup light brown sugar
⅓ cup self-rising flour
¼ tsp baking powder
3 oz/85 g milk chocolate,
 coarsely chopped

### frosting

5½ oz/150 g mascarpone cheese
¼ cup confectioners' sugar
1 tsp vanilla extract
milk or semisweet chocolate curls,
 to sprinkle

## method

**1** Preheat the oven to 375°F/190°C. Grease and line the bottom of a 12-hole mini muffin pan.

**2** Put the butter and semisweet chocolate in a heatproof bowl, set the bowl over a saucepan of gently simmering water, and heat until melted. Let the mixture stand to cool slightly.

**3** Put the egg, egg yolk, and light brown sugar in a mixing bowl and beat together with an electric whisk until the batter begins to turn frothy. Stir in the melted chocolate. Sift the flour and baking powder into the bowl, scatter in the milk chocolate, and stir together. Spoon the batter into the pan sections.

**4** Bake in the preheated oven for 12–15 minutes, or until the crust feels dry but gives a little when gently pressed. (If you're unsure, it's better to slightly undercook brownies because they lose their gooeyness when overbaked.) Let stand in the pan for 10 minutes, then transfer to a wire rack to cool.

**5** For the frosting, put the mascarpone cheese, confectioners' sugar, and vanilla in a small bowl and beat with an electric whisk until smooth and creamy. Put the mixture in a pastry bag fitted with a ½-inch/1-cm star tip and pipe swirls over the cakes. Sprinkle with chocolate curls.

# marshmallow crunch bars

## ingredients

*makes 8*

oil or melted butter,
   for greasing
1½ cups all-purpose flour
1 tbsp baking powder
¾ cup unsalted butter, softened
generous ¾ cup superfine sugar
3 eggs, beaten
1 tsp vanilla extract
scant ½ cup chopped mixed nuts
⅓ cup candied cherries,
   coarsely chopped
½ cup mini marshmallows

## method

1 Preheat the oven to 350°F/180°C. Grease and line a
   9-inch/23-cm square cake pan.

2 Sift the flour and baking powder into a large bowl and
   add the butter, sugar, eggs, and vanilla extract. Beat
   well until the mixture is smooth. Stir about two-thirds
   of the nuts and candied cherries into the mixture.

3 Spoon the mixture into the prepared pan and smooth
   level with a spatula. Sprinkle the remaining nuts and
   candied cherries and the marshmallows over the top,
   pressing down lightly.

4 Bake in the preheated oven for 40–50 minutes, or until
   risen and golden brown.

5 Let cool in the pan for about 20 minutes, until firm,
   then cut into bars and finish cooling on a wire rack.

# hazelnut bars

## ingredients

*makes 16*

⅓ cup butter, cut into small pieces,
    plus extra for greasing
1¼ cups all-purpose flour
pinch of salt
1 tsp baking powder
1 cup soft brown sugar
1 egg, beaten
4 tbsp milk
1 cup hazelnuts, halved
brown crystal sugar, for sprinkling
    (optional)

## method

*1* Preheat the oven to 350°F/180°C. Grease a 9-inch/
23-cm square cake pan and line the bottom with
baking parchment.

*2* Sift the flour, salt, and baking powder into a large
mixing bowl. Rub in the butter with your fingers until
the mixture resembles fine breadcrumbs. Stir in the
brown sugar. Add the egg, milk, and nuts to the
mixture and stir well until thoroughly combined.

*3* Spoon the mixture into the prepared cake pan and
level the surface. Sprinkle with brown sugar, if using.

*4* Bake in the preheated oven for about 25 minutes, or
until the mixture is firm to the touch when pressed
with a finger.

*5* Let cool for 10 minutes, then loosen the edges with a
round-bladed knife and turn out onto a wire rack. Cut
into squares.

# honeyed apple slices

## ingredients

*makes 12*

oil or melted butter,
    for greasing
1½ cups all-purpose flour
2 tsp baking powder
½ tsp ground allspice
¾ cup unsalted butter, softened
generous ¾ cup superfine sugar
3 eggs, beaten
1 tsp vanilla extract
2 tbsp apple juice
4 red-skinned apples
3 tbsp honey, warmed

## method

*1* Preheat the oven to 350°F/180°C. Grease and line a 12- x 9-inch/30- x 23-cm rectangular cake pan.

*2* Sift the flour, baking powder, and allspice into a large bowl and add the butter, sugar, eggs, and vanilla extract. Beat well until the mixture is smooth, then stir in the apple juice.

*3* Spoon the mixture into the prepared pan and smooth the surface with a spatula. Core and slice the apples and arrange them, overlapping, on top of the cake mixture, without pressing into the mix. Brush lightly with half the honey.

*4* Bake in the preheated oven for 30–35 minutes, or until risen, firm, and golden brown. Let cool in the pan for about 15 minutes, until firm, then cut into bars and finish cooling on a wire rack.

*5* Brush with the remaining honey before serving.

# coconut bars

## ingredients

*makes 10*

generous ½ cup butter,
    plus extra for greasing
generous 1 cup superfine sugar
2 eggs, beaten
finely grated rind of 1 orange
3 tbsp orange juice
⅔ cup sour cream
1¼ cups self-rising flour
1 cup dry unsweetened coconut
toasted long shred coconut,
    to decorate

## frosting

1 egg white
1¾ cups confectioners' sugar
1 cup dry unsweetened coconut
about 1 tbsp orange juice

## method

**1** Preheat the oven to 350°F/180°C. Grease a 9-inch/ 23-cm square cake pan and line the bottom with nonstick parchment paper.

**2** Cream together the butter and superfine sugar until pale and fluffy, then gradually beat in the eggs. Stir in the orange rind, orange juice, and sour cream. Fold in the flour and dry unsweetened coconut evenly using a metal spoon.

**3** Spoon the batter into the prepared cake pan and level the surface. Bake in the preheated oven for 35–40 minutes, or until risen and firm to the touch.

**4** Let cool for 10 minutes in the pan, then turn out and finish cooling on a wire rack.

**5** For the frosting, lightly beat the egg white, just enough to break it up, and stir in the confectioners' sugar and dry unsweetened coconut, adding enough orange juice to mix to a thick paste. Spread over the top of the cake, sprinkle with long shred coconut, then let set before slicing into bars.

# coconut lamingtons

## ingredients

*makes 16*

oil or melted butter,
    for greasing
1½ cups all-purpose flour
1 tbsp baking powder
¾ cup unsalted butter, softened
generous ¾ cup superfine
    sugar
3 eggs, beaten
1 tsp vanilla extract
2 tbsp milk
2 tbsp dry unsweetened
    coconut

### icing & coating

4½ cups confectioners' sugar
⅓ cup unsweetened cocoa
⅓ cup boiling water
5 tbsp unsalted butter,
    melted
3 cups dry unsweetened coconut

## method

**1** Preheat the oven to 350°F/180°C. Grease and line a 9-inch/23-cm square cake pan.

**2** Sift the flour and baking powder into a large bowl and add the butter, superfine sugar, eggs, and vanilla extract. Beat well until the mixture is smooth, then stir in the milk and coconut.

**3** Spoon the mixture into the prepared pan and smooth the surface with a spatula. Bake in the preheated oven for 30–35 minutes, or until firm and golden.

**4** Let cool in the pan for 10 minutes, then turn out and finish cooling on a wire rack. When the cake is cold, cut into 16 squares with a sharp knife.

**5** For the icing, sift the confectioners' sugar and cocoa into a bowl. Add the water and butter and stir until smooth. Spread out the coconut on a large plate. Dip each piece of sponge cake into the icing, holding with 2 forks to coat evenly, then toss in coconut to cover.

**6** Place on a sheet of parchment paper and let set.

## variation

For a traditional filling, cut the lamingtons in half and fill with fresh whipped heavy cream or jelly—or both.

# cinnamon squares

## ingredients

*makes 16*

1 cup butter, softened,
   plus extra for greasing
1¼ cups superfine sugar
3 eggs, lightly beaten
1¾ cups self-rising flour
½ tsp baking soda
1 tbsp ground cinnamon
⅔ cup sour cream
½ cup sunflower seeds

## method

*1* Preheat the oven to 350°F/180°C. Grease a 9-inch/ 23-cm square cake pan and line the bottom with parchment paper.

*2* In a large mixing bowl, cream together the butter and superfine sugar until light and fluffy. Gradually add the eggs, beating thoroughly after each addition. Sift the flour, baking soda, and cinnamon together into the creamed mixture and fold in evenly using a metal spoon. Spoon in the sour cream and sunflower seeds and mix gently until well combined.

*3* Spoon the batter into the prepared cake pan and smooth the surface.

*4* Bake in the preheated oven for about 45 minutes, until firm to the touch. Loosen the edges with a knife, then turn out onto a wire rack to cool completely. Slice into squares before serving.

# mango cakes

## ingredients

### makes 12

½ cup finely chopped dried mango
finely grated rind of 1 orange,
　　plus 3 tbsp juice
1 oz/25 g creamed coconut
6 tbsp lightly salted butter,
　　softened, plus extra
　　for greasing
⅓ cup superfine sugar
1 egg
⅔ cup self-rising flour
confectioners' sugar, for dusting

## method

1 Preheat the oven to 350°F/180°C. Place a 12-section silicone mini loaf pan on a baking sheet, or grease and line the bottom of individual mini loaf pans. Put the mango and orange juice in a small bowl and let stand, covered, for 2–3 hours, or until the orange juice is mostly absorbed. Finely grate the coconut (if it's firm and difficult to grate, first warm it briefly in the microwave).

2 Put the coconut, butter, sugar, egg, flour, and orange rind in a mixing bowl and beat together with an electric whisk until smooth and pale. Stir in the mango and any unabsorbed orange juice.

3 Using a teaspoon, spoon the batter into the pan sections and level with the back of the spoon. Bake in the preheated oven for 20 minutes (25 minutes if using pans), or until risen and just firm to the touch. Let rest in the pan for 5 minutes, then transfer to a wire rack to cool.

4 Serve lightly dusted with confectioners' sugar.

# chocolate

# white chocolate coffee gâteau

## ingredients

*serves 8–10*

3 tbsp unsalted butter,
    plus extra for greasing
3 oz/85 g white chocolate,
    broken into pieces
⅔ cup superfine sugar
4 extra large eggs, beaten
2 tbsp very strong black coffee
1 tsp vanilla extract
generous 1 cup all-purpose flour
white chocolate curls,
    to decorate

### frosting

6 oz/175 g white chocolate,
    broken into pieces
6 tbsp unsalted butter
generous ½ cup sour cream
generous 1 cup confectioners'
    sugar, sifted
1 tbsp coffee liqueur or very
    strong black coffee

## method

1 Preheat the oven to 350°F/180°C. Grease two 8-inch/20-cm layer cake pans and line the bottoms with parchment paper.

2 Place the butter and chocolate in a bowl set over a saucepan of hot water and leave on very low heat until just melted. Stir, then remove from the heat.

3 Place the superfine sugar, eggs, coffee, and vanilla extract in a large bowl set over a saucepan of hot water and whisk hard with an electric whisk until the mixture is pale and thick. Remove from the heat, sift in the flour and fold in lightly. Fold in the butter and chocolate mixture, then divide the batter between the prepared pans. Bake in the preheated oven for 25–30 minutes, until golden brown, and springy to the touch. Cool in the pans for 2 minutes, then run a knife around the edges to loosen and turn out onto a wire rack to cool.

4 For the frosting, place the chocolate and butter in a bowl set over a saucepan of hot water and heat gently until melted. Remove from the heat, stir in the sour cream, then add the confectioners' sugar and coffee liqueur. Chill the frosting for at least 30 minutes, stirring occasionally, until it becomes thick and glossy. Sandwich the cakes together with some of the frosting and spread the rest over the top and sides. Arrange the chocolate curls over the top of the cake and let set.

# rich chocolate rum torte

## ingredients

*serves 8*

oil or melted butter,
    for greasing
2¹/₂ oz/70 g semisweet
    chocolate, broken into pieces
2 tbsp milk
1¹/₂ cups all-purpose flour
1 tbsp baking powder
³/₄ cup unsalted butter,
    softened
generous ³/₄ cup dark
    brown sugar
3 eggs, beaten
1 tsp vanilla extract
chocolate curls or grated
    chocolate, to decorate

### frosting

8 oz/225 g semisweet
    chocolate, broken into pieces
1 cup heavy cream
2 tbsp dark rum

## method

*1* Preheat the oven to 350°F/180°C. Grease three 7-inch/18-cm layer cake pans and line the bottoms with parchment paper.

*2* Put the chocolate and milk into a small pan and heat gently, without boiling, until melted. Stir and remove from the heat.

*3* Sift the flour and baking powder into a large bowl and add the butter, sugar, eggs, and vanilla extract. Beat well until smooth, then stir in the chocolate mixture.

*4* Divide the cake batter among the prepared pans and smooth level. Bake in the preheated oven for 20–25 minutes, or until risen and firm to the touch. Let cool in the pans for 5 minutes, then turn out onto wire racks to finish cooling.

*5* For the filling and frosting, melt the chocolate with the cream and rum in a small pan over low heat. Remove from the heat and let cool, stirring occasionally, until it reaches a spreadable consistency.

*6* Sandwich the cakes together with about a third of the frosting, then spread the remainder over the top and sides of the cake, swirling with a spatula. Sprinkle with chocolate curls and let set.

# chocolate & almond layer cake

## ingredients

*serves 10–12*

oil or melted butter,
    for greasing
7 eggs
1¾ cups superfine sugar
1¼ cups all-purpose flour
½ cup unsweetened cocoa
4 tbsp butter, melted
½ cup toasted slivered almonds,
    crushed lightly and grated
    chocolate, to decorate

### filling & topping

7 oz/200 g semisweet
    chocolate, broken into pieces
½ cup butter
4 tbsp confectioners' sugar

## method

1 Preheat the oven to 350°F/180°C. Grease a deep
   9-inch/23-cm square cake pan and line the bottom
   with parchment paper.

2 Beat the eggs and superfine sugar in a mixing bowl
   with an electric mixer for about 10 minutes, or until
   the batter is very light and foamy and the beaters
   leave a trail that lasts a few seconds when lifted.

3 Sift the flour and cocoa together and fold half into
   the batter. Drizzle over the melted butter and fold the
   rest of the flour and cocoa into the mixture. Pour into
   the prepared pan and bake in a preheated oven for
   30–35 minutes, or until springy to the touch. Let cool
   in the pan for 5 minutes, then turn out onto a wire rack
   to finish cooling.

4 For the filling and topping, melt the chocolate and
   butter together, then remove from the heat. Stir in the
   confectioners' sugar and let cool, then beat until thick
   enough to spread.

5 Halve the cake lengthwise and cut each half into
   3 layers. Sandwich the layers together with
   three-quarters of the chocolate mixture. Spread the
   remainder over the cake and mark a wavy pattern on
   the top. Press the almonds onto the sides. Decorate
   with grated chocolate.

# chocolate & cherry gâteau

## ingredients

*serves 8*

oil or melted butter,
   for greasing
1¹⁄₃ cups all-purpose flour
2 tbsp unsweetened cocoa
1 tbsp baking powder
³⁄₄ cup unsalted butter,
   softened
generous ³⁄₄ cup
   superfine sugar
3 eggs, beaten
1 tsp vanilla extract
2 tbsp milk
3 tbsp Kirsch or brandy (optional)
grated chocolate and fresh whole
   cherries, to decorate

### filling & topping

2 cups heavy cream
2 tbsp confectioners' sugar
1¹⁄₃ cups fresh or frozen pitted
   black cherries

## method

1 Preheat the oven to 350°F/180°C. Grease two 8-inch/ 20-cm layer cake pans and line the bottoms with parchment paper.

2 Sift the flour, cocoa, and baking powder into a large bowl and add the butter, superfine sugar, eggs, and vanilla extract. Beat well until the mixture is smooth and stir in the milk.

3 Divide the mixture between the prepared pans and smooth level. Bake in the preheated oven for 25–30 minutes, or until risen and firm to the touch. Let cool in the pans for 2–3 minutes, then turn out onto wire racks to finish cooling.

4 When the cakes are cold, sprinkle with the Kirsch, if using. Whip the cream with the confectioners' sugar until thick, then spread about a third over the top of one of the cakes. Spread the cherries among the cream mixture and place the second cake on top.

5 Spread the remaining cream mixture over the top and sides of the cake and decorate with grated chocolate and fresh whole cherries.

# black forest roulade

## ingredients

*serves 8–10*

sunflower oil, for greasing
6 oz/175 g semisweet chocolate
2–3 tbsp Kirsch or cognac
5 eggs
1 cup superfine sugar
confectioners' sugar, for dusting

### filling

1½ cups heavy cream
1 tbsp Kirsch or cognac
12 oz/350 g fresh black cherries,
     pitted, or 14 oz/400 g
     canned sour cherries, drained
     and pitted

## method

*1* Preheat the oven to 375°F/190°C. Lightly oil and line a 14- x 10-inch/35- x 25-cm jelly roll pan with parchment paper.

*2* Break the chocolate into small pieces and place in a heatproof bowl set over a saucepan of gently simmering water. Add the Kirsch and heat gently, stirring until the mixture is smooth. Remove from the pan and set aside.

*3* Place the eggs and superfine sugar in a large heatproof bowl and set over the pan of gently simmering water. Whisk the eggs and sugar until very thick and creamy. Remove from the heat and whisk in the cooled chocolate mixture.

*4* Spoon into the prepared jelly roll pan, then tap the pan lightly on a counter to smooth the top. Bake in the preheated oven for 20 minutes, or until firm to the touch. Remove from the oven and immediately invert onto a sheet of parchment paper that has been dusted with confectioners' sugar. Lift off the pan and its lining paper, then roll up, encasing the new parchment paper in the roulade. Let stand until cooled.

*5* For the filling, whip the cream until soft peaks form, then stir in the Kirsch. Unroll the roulade and spread over the cream to within ¼ inch/5 mm of the edges. Scatter the cherries over the cream. Carefully roll up the roulade again and place on a serving platter.

# double chocolate mint sponge

## ingredients

### serves 8

oil or melted butter,
    for greasing
generous 1¼ cups all-purpose
    flour
2 tbsp unsweetened cocoa
1 tbsp baking powder
¾ cup unsalted butter,
    softened
scant 1 cup superfine sugar
3 eggs, beaten
1 tbsp milk
12 chocolate mint sticks,
    chopped
⅔ cup chocolate spread,
    plus extra to drizzle
chocolate mint sticks,
    to decorate

## method

*1* Preheat the oven to 350°F/180°C. Grease two 8-inch/ 20-cm layer cake pans and line the bottoms with parchment paper.

*2* Sift the flour, unsweetened cocoa, and baking powder into a bowl and beat in the butter, sugar, and eggs, mixing until smooth. Stir in the milk and chocolate mint pieces.

*3* Spread the batter into the pans. Bake for 25–30 minutes until risen and firm. Cool in the pan for 2 minutes, then turn out onto a wire rack to finish cooling.

*4* Sandwich the cakes together with the chocolate spread, then drizzle more chocolate spread over the top. Decorate the cake with chocolate mint sticks.

# hot chocolate cheesecake

## ingredients

*serves 8–10*

oil or melted butter,
    for greasing
scant 1½ cups all-purpose flour
2 tbsp unsweetened cocoa
4 tbsp butter, plus extra
    for greasing
2 tbsp superfine sugar
¼ cup ground almonds
1 egg yolk
confectioners' sugar and
    grated chocolate, to decorate

### filling

2 eggs, separated
scant ½ cup superfine sugar
1½ cups cream cheese
4 tbsp ground almonds
⅔ cup heavy cream
¼ cup unsweetened cocoa,
    sifted
1 tsp vanilla extract

## method

*1* Grease an 8-inch/20-cm loose-bottom round cake pan

*2* Sift the flour and cocoa into a bowl and rub in the butter until the mixture resembles fine breadcrumbs. Stir in the sugar and ground almonds. Add the egg yolk and enough water to make a soft dough.

*3* Roll the pastry out on a lightly floured work surface and use to line the prepared pan. Let chill for 30 minutes. Preheat the oven to 325°F/160°C.

*4* For the filling, put the egg yolks and sugar in a large bowl and beat until thick and pale. Beat in the cream cheese, ground almonds, cream, cocoa, and vanilla extract until well combined.

*5* Put the egg whites in a large bowl and beat until stiff but not dry. Stir a little of the egg white into the cream cheese mixture, then fold in the remainder. Pour into the pastry shell.

*6* Bake in the preheated oven for 1½ hours, until well risen and just firm to the touch. Let cool slightly, then carefully remove from the pan, dust with confectioner sugar, and sprinkle with grated chocolate. Serve warm

# chocolate cake with syrup

## ingredients

### serves 12

oil or melted butter,
    for greasing
8 oz/225 g semisweet
    chocolate, broken
    into pieces
½ cup butter
1 tbsp strong black coffee
4 large eggs
2 egg yolks
⅔ cup superfine sugar
½ cup all-purpose flour
2 tsp ground cinnamon
1 cup ground almonds
chocolate-covered coffee
    beans, to decorate

### syrup

1¼ cups strong black coffee
⅔ cup superfine sugar
1 cinnamon stick

## method

1 Preheat the oven to 375°F/190°C. Grease an 8-inch/
    20-cm round cake pan and line with parchment paper

2 Place the chocolate, butter, and coffee in a heatproof
    bowl and set over a saucepan of gently simmering
    water until melted. Stir to blend, then remove from the
    heat and let cool slightly.

3 Place the whole eggs, egg yolks, and sugar in a
    separate bowl and beat together until thick and pale.
    Sift the flour and cinnamon over the egg mixture.
    Add the almonds and the chocolate mixture and fold
    in carefully. Spoon the cake batter into the prepared
    pan. Bake in the preheated oven for 35 minutes, or
    until the tip of a knife inserted into the center comes
    out clean. Let cool slightly before turning out onto a
    serving plate.

4 For the syrup, place the coffee, sugar, and cinnamon
    stick in a heavy-bottom pan and heat gently, stirring,
    until the sugar has dissolved. Increase the heat and bc
    for 5 minutes, or until reduced and thickened slightly.
    Keep warm. Pierce the surface of the cake with a
    skewer, then drizzle half the coffee syrup over the top.
    Decorate with chocolate-covered coffee beans. Cut
    into wedges, drizzle with remaining coffee syrup,
    and serve.

# chocolate sandwich cake

## ingredients

*serves 8*

oil or melted butter,
    for greasing
1⅓ cups all-purpose flour
2 tbsp unsweetened cocoa
1 tbsp baking powder
¾ cup unsalted butter,
    softened
generous ¾ cup superfine sugar
3 eggs, beaten
1 tsp vanilla extract
2 tbsp milk
⅔ cup chocolate spread
confectioners' sugar,
    for dusting

## method

*1* Preheat the oven to 350°F/180°C. Grease two 8-inch/
20-cm layer cake pans and line the bottoms with
parchment paper.

*2* Sift the flour, cocoa, and baking powder into a large
bowl and add the butter, superfine sugar, eggs, and
vanilla extract. Beat well until the mixture is smooth,
then stir in the milk.

*3* Divide the batter between the prepared pans and
smooth level. Bake in the preheated oven for 25–30
minutes, or until golden brown and firm to the touch.
Let cool in the pans for 2–3 minutes, then turn out
onto a wire rack to finish cooling.

*4* When the cakes have cooled completely, sandwich
them together with the chocolate spread, then dust
with confectioners' sugar and serve.

## variation

For a more luxurious cake, replace the chocolate spread
filling and confectioners' sugar dusting with 1¼ cups of
whipped heavy cream. Before serving, arrange sliced
strawberries on the top.

# dotty chocolate chip cake

## ingredients

### serves 10

soft margarine or softened butter, plus extra for greasing
scant 1 cup superfine sugar
3 eggs, beaten
1½ tsp baking powder
2 tbsp unsweetened cocoa
⅓ cup white chocolate chips

### frosting

6 oz/175 g milk chocolate or semisweet chocolate, broken into pieces
scant ½ cup unsalted butter or margarine
1 tbsp dark corn syrup
1½ oz/40 g small colored candies

## method

1 Preheat the oven to 325°F/160°C. Grease an 8-inch/20-cm round cake pan and line the bottom with parchment paper.

2 Place the margarine, sugar, eggs, flour, baking powder, and cocoa in a bowl and beat until just smooth. Stir in the chocolate chips, mixing evenly.

3 Spoon the batter into the prepared pan and spread the top level. Bake in the preheated oven for 40–45 minutes, until risen and firm to the touch. Cool in the pan for 5 minutes, then turn out and finish cooling completely on a wire rack.

4 For the frosting, place the chocolate, butter, and corn syrup in a saucepan over low heat and stir until just melted and smooth.

5 Remove from the heat and let cool until it begins to thicken enough to leave a trail when the spoon is lifted. Pour the frosting over the top of the cake, letting it drizzle down the sides. Arrange the candies over the top of the cake.

# marbled chocolate & vanilla ring

## ingredients

*serves 12*

oil or melted butter,
    for greasing
1½ cups all-purpose flour
1 tbsp baking powder
¾ cup unsalted butter, softened
generous ¾ cup superfine sugar
3 eggs, beaten
2 tbsp unsweetened cocoa
2 tbsp milk
1 tsp vanilla extract
confectioners' sugar, for dusting

## method

*1* Preheat the oven to 160°C/325°F. Grease a 1.5-liter/
2¾-pint ring cake tin, preferably non-stick.

*2* Sift the flour and baking powder into a large bowl and
add the butter, caster sugar and eggs. Beat well until
the mixture is smooth. Transfer half the mixture to a
separate bowl.

*3* Mix the cocoa powder with the milk and stir into one
bowl of mixture. Add the vanilla extract to the other
bowl and mix evenly. Spoon alternate tablespoons of
the two mixtures into the prepared tin and swirl lightly
with a palette knife for a marbled effect.

*4* Bake in the preheated oven for 40–50 minutes, or until
risen, firm and golden brown. Leave to cool in the tin
for 10 minutes, then turn out and finish cooling on a
wire rack. Dust with icing sugar before serving.

# chocolate ganache cake

## ingredients

*serves 10*

¾ cup butter, plus extra for
   greasing
¾ cup superfine sugar
4 eggs, lightly beaten
1¾ cups self-rising flour
1 tbsp unsweetened cocoa
1¾ oz/50 g semisweet chocolate,
   melted

### ganache

2 cups heavy cream
13 oz/375 g semisweet chocolate,
   broken into pieces
7 oz/200 g chocolate-flavored
   cake covering, to finish

## method

**1** Preheat the oven to 350°F/180°C. Lightly grease and base-line an 8-inch/20-cm springform cake pan. Beat the butter and sugar until light and fluffy. Gradually add the eggs, beating well. Sift the flour and cocoa together. Fold into the cake mixture. Fold in the melted chocolate.

**2** Spoon into the cake pan, and bake in the preheated oven for 40 minutes, or until springy to the touch. Let cool for 5 minutes in the pan, then turn out onto a wire rack to cool. Cut the cold cake into two layers.

**3** To make the ganache, place the cream in a pan and bring to a boil, stirring. Add the chocolate and stir until melted and combined. Pour into a bowl and whip for about 5 minutes, or until fluffy and cool. Set aside one-third of the ganache and use the rest to sandwich the cake together and spread smoothly and evenly over the top and sides of the cake.

**4** Melt the cake covering and spread it over a large sheet of baking parchment. Let cool until just set. Cut into strips a little wider than the height of the cake. Place them around the edge of the cake, overlapping slightly.

**5** Using a pastry bag fitted with a fine tip, pipe the reserved ganache in tear drops or shells to cover the top of the cake. Let chill in the refrigerator for 1 hour before serving.

# warm white chocolate macadamia ring

## ingredients

*serves 8*

oil or melted butter, for greasing
2½ oz/70 g white chocolate,
    broken into pieces
2 tbsp milk
1 tsp vanilla extract
1½ cups all-purpose flour
1 tbsp baking powder
¾ cup unsalted butter, softened
generous ¾ cup superfine sugar
3 eggs, beaten
½ cup finely chopped macadamia
    nuts, plus extra to decorate

**sauce**

3½ oz/100 g white chocolate,
    broken into pieces
½ cup light cream
½ tsp vanilla extract

## method

*1* Preheat the oven to 350°F/180°C. Grease a 6¾-cup tube cake pan, preferably nonstick.

*2* Put the white chocolate, milk, and vanilla extract into a small pan and heat gently, stirring occasionally, until just melted and smooth. Remove from the heat.

*3* Sift the flour and baking powder into a large bowl and add the butter, sugar, and eggs. Beat well until the mixture is smooth, then beat in the melted chocolate mixture. Stir in the chopped nuts, mixing evenly.

*4* Spoon the mixture into the prepared pan and smooth the surface with a spatula. Bake in the preheated oven for 35–40 minutes, or until the cake is risen, firm, and golden brown.

*5* Meanwhile, make the sauce. Put the chocolate, cream, and vanilla extract into a pan and heat gently until melted and smooth. Keep warm.

*6* Let the cake cool in the pan for 2–3 minutes, then turn out carefully onto a warmed serving plate. Drizzle the warm sauce over the cake and sprinkle with nuts, then serve in thick slices.

# gooey orange chocolate chip cake

## ingredients

**serves 6**

oil or melted butter,
    for greasing
2 oranges
1½ cups all-purpose flour
2 tsp baking powder
¾ cup unsalted butter, softened
generous ¾ cup superfine sugar
3 eggs, beaten
1 tsp vanilla extract
generous ½ cup semisweet
    chocolate chips

**sauce**

3 oz/85 g semisweet chocolate
3 tbsp unsalted butter
3 tbsp orange juice

## method

*1* Preheat the oven to 350°F/180°C. Grease and line a 9-inch/23-cm square cake pan.

*2* Finely grate the rind from 1 orange and reserve. Use a sharp knife to cut off all the peel and white pith from both oranges and carefully remove the segments. Chop half the segments into small pieces.

*3* Sift the flour and baking powder into a large bowl and add the butter, sugar, eggs, and vanilla extract. Beat well until the mixture is smooth, then stir in the reserved orange rind and chopped orange.

*4* Spoon the mixture into the prepared pan and smooth the surface with a spatula. Sprinkle the chocolate chips over the top, spreading to the edges. Bake in the preheated oven for 35–40 minutes, or until risen, firm, and golden brown.

*5* For the sauce, put the chocolate, butter, and orange juice into a pan and heat gently, stirring, until melted and smooth. Serve the cake warm, topped with the reserved orange segments and with the sauce spooned over the top.

# chocolate mint cake pops

## ingredients

*makes 26–28*

10½ oz/300 g semisweet
    chocolate, coarsely chopped
2 tbsp unsalted butter, softened
1¾ oz/50 g hard mint candies
1 lb/450 g milk chocolate
1 cup coarsely chopped mini
    marshmallows
26–28 x 2½-inch/6-cm
    lollipop sticks
chocolate sprinkles, to decorate

## method

*1* Line a baking sheet with parchment paper. Put the semisweet chocolate in a heatproof bowl, set the bowl over a saucepan of gently simmering water, and heat until melted. Stir in the butter. Let stand until the mixture is cool but not beginning to set.

*2* Put the mint candies in a plastic bag and tap firmly with a rolling pin until they are broken into tiny pieces. Finely chop 5½ oz/150 g of the milk chocolate, then stir it into the melted semisweet chocolate with the mints and marshmallows until thoroughly mixed.

*3* As soon as the mixture is firm enough to hold its shape, divide and roll into 26–28 even balls. Place the balls on the baking sheet and chill in the refrigerator for 30–60 minutes, until firm but not brittle. Push a lollipop stick into each cake pop, then chill for an additional 10 minutes.

*4* Coarsely chop the remaining milk chocolate and melt as above, then remove from the heat. Dip a cake pop into the chocolate, turning it until coated. Lift it from the bowl, letting the excess drip back into the bowl, and place it in a cup or glass. Sprinkle with the chocolate sprinkles. Repeat with the remaining cake pops. Chill or let stand in a cool place until the chocolate has set.

# mont blanc macaroons

## ingredients

*makes 6*

3/4 cup ground almonds
scant 1 cup confectioners' sugar,
    plus extra for dusting
2 tbsp unsweetened cocoa
2 extra large egg whites
1/4 cup superfine sugar

### filling

1 cup heavy cream
1/4 cup sweetened chestnut
    puree
2 tbsp semisweet chocolate
    shavings

## method

*1* Place the ground almonds, confectioners' sugar, and cocoa in a food processor and process for 15 seconds. Sift the mixture into a bowl. Line 2 baking sheets with parchment paper.

*2* Place the egg whites in a large bowl and whip until holding soft peaks. Gradually beat in the superfine sugar to make a firm, glossy meringue. Using a spatula, fold the almond mixture into the meringue one-third at a time. When all the dry ingredients are thoroughly incorporated, continue to fold the mixture until it forms a shiny batter with a thick, ribbonlike consistency.

*3* Pour the batter into a pastry bag fitted with a 1/2-inch/1-cm plain tip. Pipe 12 large circles onto the prepared baking sheets. Tap the baking sheets firmly onto a work surface to remove air bubbles. Let stand for 30 minutes. Preheat the oven to 325°F/160°C.

*4* Bake in the preheated oven for 15–20 minutes. Cool for 10 minutes. Carefully peel the macaroons off the parchment paper and let cool completely.

*5* For the filling, whip the cream until holding soft peaks and fold into the chestnut puree. Pipe the chestnut mixture onto half the macaroons. Top with chocolate shavings and the remaining macaroon shells. Serve dusted with confectioners' sugar.

# chocolate whoopie pies

## ingredients

*makes 10*

1¼ cups all-purpose flour
1½ tsp baking soda
scant ½ cup unsweetened cocoa
large pinch of salt
6 tbsp butter, softened
generous ⅓ cup vegetable
    shortening
¾ cup dark brown sugar
1 large egg, beaten
1 tsp vanilla extract
⅔ cup milk

### filling

8 oz/225 g white marshmallows
4 tbsp milk
½ cup vegetable shortening
½ cup confectioners' sugar, sifted

## method

**1** Preheat the oven to 350°F/180°C. Line 2–3 large cookie sheets with parchment paper. Sift the all-purpose flour, baking soda, unsweetened cocoa, and salt.

**2** Place the butter, vegetable shortening, and sugar in a large bowl and beat with an electric mixer until pale and fluffy. Beat in the egg and vanilla extract followed by half of the flour mixture and then the milk. Stir in the rest of the flour mixture and mix thoroughly.

**3** Pipe or spoon 20 mounds of the batter onto the prepared cookie sheets, spaced well apart to allow for spreading. Bake in the preheated oven, one sheet at a time, for 12–14 minutes until risen and just firm to the touch. Cool for 5 minutes, then using a palette knife transfer to a wire rack and let cool completely.

**4** For the filling, place the marshmallows and milk in a heatproof bowl set over a pan of simmering water. Heat until the marshmallows have melted, stirring occasionally. Remove from the heat and let cool. Place the vegetable shortening and confectioners' sugar in a bowl and beat together until smooth and creamy. Add the creamed mixture to the marshmallow and beat for 1–2 minutes until fluffy.

**5** To assemble, spread the filling over the flat side of half the cakes. Top with the remaining cakes.

# chocolate & lime whoopie pies

## ingredients

### makes 10

generous 1¾ cups
    all-purpose flour
1 tsp baking soda
¼ cup unsweetened cocoa
large pinch of salt
½ cup butter, softened
¾ cup superfine sugar
1 large egg, beaten
1 tsp vanilla extract
4 tbsp sour cream
3 tbsp milk

### filling

¾ cup cream cheese
5 tbsp unsalted butter, softened
finely grated zest and juice of
    1 lime
1 cup confectioners' sugar, sifted

### icing

3 oz/85 g semisweet chocolate,
    broken into pieces
4 tbsp unsalted butter

## method

*1* Preheat the oven to 350°F/180°C. Line 2–3 large cookie sheets with parchment paper. Sift the all-purpose flour, baking soda, unsweetened cocoa, and salt.

*2* Place the butter and sugar in a large bowl and beat with an electric mixer until pale and fluffy. Beat in the egg and vanilla extract followed by half of the flour and then the sour cream and milk. Stir in the rest of the flour mixture and mix until thoroughly incorporated.

*3* Pipe or spoon 20 mounds of the batter onto the prepared cookie sheets, spaced well apart to allow for spreading. Bake one sheet at a time, in the preheated oven, for 10–12 minutes until risen and just firm to the touch. Cool for 5 minutes, then using a palette knife transfer to a wire rack and let cool completely.

*4* For the filling, place the cream cheese, butter, lime zest juice, and sugar in a bowl and beat with an electric mixer until smooth. To assemble, spread the lime filling on the flat side of half the cakes. Top with the rest of the cakes.

*5* For the icing, place the chocolate and butter in a heatproof bowl set over a pan of simmering water and heat until melted, stirring occasionally. Remove from the heat and let cool for 20 minutes. Gently dip one half of each whoopie pie in the chocolate icing and let cool.

# chocolate chip whoopie pies

## ingredients

*makes 10*

generous 1¾ cups all-purpose
    flour
1 tsp baking soda
large pinch of salt
½ cup butter, softened
¾ cup light brown sugar
1 large egg, beaten
1 tsp vanilla extract
⅔ cup sour cream
3 oz/85 g semisweet
    chocolate chips

### filling

5½ oz/150 g semisweet chocolate,
    broken into pieces
½ cup unsalted butter, softened
⅔ cup heavy cream

## method

*1* Preheat the oven to 350°F/180°C. Line 2–3 large
    cookie sheets with parchment paper. Sift together the
    all-purpose flour, baking soda, and salt.

*2* Place the butter and sugar in a large bowl and beat
    with an electric mixer until pale and fluffy. Beat in the
    egg and vanilla extract, followed by half of the flour
    mixture and then the sour cream. Stir in the rest of the
    flour mixture and mix until thoroughly incorporated.
    Stir in half of the chocolate chips

*3* Pipe or spoon 20 mounds of the batter onto the
    prepared cookie sheets, spaced well apart to allow for
    spreading. Sprinkle over the rest of the chocolate chips
    Bake in the preheated oven, one sheet at a time, for
    10–12 minutes until risen and just firm to the touch.
    Cool for 5 minutes, then using a palette knife transfer
    to a wire rack and let cool completely.

*4* For the filling, place the chocolate and butter in a
    heatproof bowl set over a pan of simmering water and
    heat until melted, stirring occasionally. Remove from
    the heat and let cool for 20 minutes. Stir the cream into
    the cooled chocolate, then chill in the refrigerator for
    10–15 minutes until firm enough to spread.

*5* To assemble, spread or pipe the chocolate filling on the
    flat side of half of the cakes. Top with the rest of the cakes

fruit

# berry crunch cake

## ingredients

*serves 8*

oil or melted butter,
    for greasing
1½ cups all-purpose flour,
    plus 1 tbsp
2 tsp baking powder
¾ cup unsalted butter, softened
generous ¾ cup superfine sugar
3 eggs, beaten
1 tsp vanilla extract
2 cups fresh mixed berries, such
    as raspberries, blueberries,
    and blackberries
1¼ cups crushed gingersnaps

## method

1 Preheat the oven to 350°F/180°C. Grease and line the bottom of a 9-inch/23-cm round springform cake pan.

2 Sift the 1½ cups flour and the baking powder into a large bowl and add the butter, sugar, eggs, and vanilla extract. Beat well until the mixture is smooth.

3 Spoon about half the mixture into the prepared pan and smooth the surface with a spatula. Spread the berries evenly over the mixture. Stir the extra tablespoon of flour into the remaining mix. Spread out the crushed cookies on a large plate. Using two spoons, coat small spoonfuls of the mix in the crushed cookies, then arrange over the cake. Sprinkle over any remaining cookie crumbs.

4 Bake in the preheated oven for 45–55 minutes, or until risen, firm, and golden brown. Let cool in the pan for 2–3 minutes, then remove the sides and finish cooling on a wire rack. Best eaten on the day of making.

# frosted raspberry almond ring

## ingredients

*serves 8–10*

oil or melted butter,
    for greasing
1½ cups all-purpose flour
1 tbsp baking powder
¾ cup unsalted butter, softened
generous ¾ cup superfine sugar
3 eggs, beaten
1 tsp almond extract
⅔ cup ground almonds
1⅓ cups fresh raspberries
toasted slivered almonds,
    to decorate

### frosting

1 extra large egg white
1¼ cups confectioners' sugar
1 tbsp dark corn syrup
¼ tsp cream of tartar

## method

1 Preheat the oven to 325°F/160°C. Grease a 6¾-cup tube cake pan, preferably nonstick.

2 Sift the flour and baking powder into a large bowl and add the butter, superfine sugar, eggs, and almond extract. Beat well until the mixture is smooth, then stir in the ground almonds. Mash half the raspberries with a fork and stir into the mixture.

3 Spoon the mixture into the prepared pan and smooth the surface with a spatula. Bake in the preheated oven for 40–45 minutes, or until the cake is risen, firm, and golden brown.

4 Let cool in the pan for 10 minutes, then turn out carefully onto a wire rack to finish cooling.

5 For the frosting, place the egg white, confectioners' sugar, corn syrup, and cream of tartar in a bowl over a pan of hot water and whisk vigorously with an electric mixer until thick enough to hold its shape.

6 Swirl the frosting over the cake. Decorate with the remaining raspberries and the slivered almonds.

# raspberry & chocolate meringue

## ingredients

*serves 10*

3 egg whites
¾ cup superfine sugar
1 tsp cornstarch
1 oz/25 g semisweet chocolate,
   grated

### filling & topping

6 oz/175 g semisweet chocolate,
   broken into pieces
2 cups heavy cream, whipped
2 cups fresh raspberries
a little melted chocolate,
   to decorate

## method

*1* Preheat the oven to 275°F/140°C. Draw three rectangles measuring 4 x 10 inches/10 x 25 cm, on sheets of parchment paper and place on two cookie sheets.

*2* Whisk the egg whites in a mixing bowl until soft peaks form, then gradually whisk in half of the sugar and continue whisking until the mixture is very stiff and glossy. Carefully fold in the remaining sugar, the cornstarch, and the grated chocolate with a metal spoon or a spatula. Spoon the meringue mixture into a pastry bag fitted with a ½-inch/1-cm plain tip and pipe lines across the rectangles.

*3* Bake in the preheated oven for 1½ hours. Turn off the oven and let the meringues cool inside the oven, then peel away the parchment paper.

*4* Place the chocolate in a heatproof bowl set over a pan of gently simmering water until melted. Spread the chocolate over two of the meringue layers. Let set. Place one meringue layer on a plate and top with about one third of the cream and raspberries. Gently place the second meringue layer on top and spread with half of the remaining cream and raspberries. Place the last meringue layer on the top and decorate with the remaining cream and raspberries. Drizzle the melted chocolate over the top and serve.

# strawberry sponge slices

## ingredients

*serves 6–8*

oil or melted butter,
　for greasing
1⅓ cups all-purpose flour
1½ tsp baking powder
¾ cup unsalted butter, softened
generous ¾ cup superfine sugar
3 eggs, beaten
1 tsp vanilla extract
2 tbsp milk
scant 2 cups fresh strawberries
generous 1 cup mascarpone
　cheese
confectioners' sugar,
　for dusting

## method

1 Preheat the oven to 350°F/180°C. Grease and line a 9- x 13-inch/23- x 33-cm jelly roll pan with the paper ½ inch/1 cm above the rim.

2 Sift the flour and baking powder into a large bowl and add the butter, superfine sugar, eggs, and vanilla extract. Beat well until the mixture is smooth, then beat in the milk.

3 Spoon the mixture into the prepared pan and smooth into the corners with a spatula. Bake in the preheated oven for 15–20 minutes, or until risen, firm, and golden brown. Let cool in the pan.

4 When the cake is cold, cut crosswise into three rectangles. Hull and chop the strawberries, reserving 4–5 for decoration. Stir the chopped strawberries into the mascarpone and use the soft cheese to sandwich together the cakes.

5 To serve, dust the cake with confectioners' sugar. Hull and slice the reserved strawberries and arrange on top

# strawberry mousse cake

## ingredients

*serves 8–10*

oil or melted butter,
    for greasing
1½ cups all-purpose flour
1 tbsp baking powder
¾ cup unsalted butter, softened
generous ¾ cup superfine
    sugar
3 eggs, beaten
1 tsp vanilla extract
2 tbsp milk

### filling & topping

4 tsp powdered gelatin
3 tbsp orange juice
5 cups fresh strawberries
3 tbsp superfine sugar
1½ cups heavy cream
scant ½ cup grape jelly,
    warmed

## method

**1** Preheat the oven to 325°F/160°C. Grease a 9-inch/23-cm round springform cake pan and line with parchment paper.

**2** Sift the flour and baking powder into a large bowl and add the butter, sugar, eggs, and vanilla extract. Beat well until the batter is smooth, then stir in the milk.

**3** Spoon the batter into the prepared pan and smooth level. Bake in the preheated oven for 45–55 minutes, or until risen and golden brown.

**4** Let cool in the pan for 5 minutes, then turn out onto a wire rack to finish cooling. Cut the cake in half horizontally and place half back in the cake pan.

**5** For the filling, dissolve the gelatin in the orange juice in a small bowl placed in a pan of hot water. In a blender or processor, puree 3½ cups of the strawberries with the sugar. Whip the cream until thick enough to hold its shape. Quickly stir the gelatin into the strawberry mixture, then fold in the cream.

**6** Pour the mixture into the cake pan and place the second half of the cake on top. Chill in the refrigerator until set. Turn out the cake and spread the top with warmed grape jelly. Decorate the mousse cake with the remaining strawberries.

# blueberry orange streusel cake

## ingredients

*serves 8–10*

oil or melted butter,
    for greasing
1½ cups all-purpose flour
2 tsp baking powder
¾ cup unsalted butter, softened
generous ¾ cup superfine sugar
3 eggs, beaten
1 tsp vanilla extract
finely grated rind of ½ orange
½ cup ground almonds
generous 1 cup fresh blueberries

### topping

½ cup all-purpose flour
2 tbsp unsalted butter, softened
2 tbsp superfine sugar
finely grated rind of ½ orange

## method

1 Preheat the oven to 325°F/160°C. Grease and line the bottom of a 9-inch/23-cm round springform cake pan.

2 For the topping, put all the ingredients into a bowl and mix with a fork to make a crumbly mixture.

3 Sift the flour and baking powder into a large bowl and add the butter, sugar, eggs, and vanilla extract. Beat well until the mixture is smooth, then add the orange rind, ground almonds, and half the blueberries.

4 Spoon the mixture into the prepared pan, smooth level with a spatula, and sprinkle with the remaining blueberries. Spread the crumble topping evenly over the top, covering completely.

5 Bake in the preheated oven for 1–1¼ hours, or until risen, firm, and golden brown. Let cool in the pan for 10 minutes, then remove the sides of the pan and finish cooling on a wire rack.

# pear & hazelnut streusel cake

## ingredients

*serves 8*

oil or melted butter,
   for greasing
1½ cups all-purpose flour
2 tsp baking powder
¾ cup unsalted butter, softened
generous ¾ cup superfine sugar
3 eggs, beaten
1 tsp vanilla extract
½ cup ground hazelnuts
2 firm ripe pears, peeled, cored,
   and finely chopped

### streusel topping

scant ½ cup finely chopped
   toasted hazelnuts
scant ¼ cup dark brown sugar
3 tbsp all-purpose flour
½ tsp ground cinnamon
2 tbsp unsalted butter, melted

## method

1 Preheat the oven to 350°F/180°C. Grease and line a 9-inch/23-cm round springform cake pan.

2 For the streusel topping, combine the chopped hazelnuts, brown sugar, flour, cinnamon, and butter in a small bowl with a fork to make a crumbly mixture.

3 Sift the flour and baking powder into a large bowl and add the butter, superfine sugar, eggs, and vanilla extract. Beat well until the mixture is smooth, then stir in the ground hazelnuts and half the pears.

4 Spoon the mixture into the prepared pan and smooth the surface with a spatula. Sprinkle the remaining pears over the top and spread level. Sprinkle the streusel topping evenly over the cake.

5 Bake in the preheated oven for about 1 hour, or until risen and firm. Let cool in the pan for 2–3 minutes, then remove the sides of the pan and finish cooling on a wire rack.

# peachy oat crumble cake

## ingredients

*serves 8–10*

oil or melted butter,
    for greasing
1½ cups all-purpose flour
1 tbsp baking powder
1 tsp ground star anise
¾ cup unsalted butter, softened
generous ¾ cup superfine sugar
3 eggs, beaten
1 tsp vanilla extract
4 ripe peaches, pitted and
    coarsely chopped

## topping

1¼ cups rolled oats
generous ¼ cup superfine sugar
4 tbsp unsalted butter

## method

*1* Preheat the oven to 350°F/180°C. Grease and line the bottom of a 10-inch/25-cm round springform cake pan.

*2* Sift the flour, baking powder, and star anise into a large bowl and add the butter, sugar, eggs, and vanilla extract. Beat well until the mixture is smooth.

*3* Spoon the mixture into the prepared pan and smooth the surface with a spatula. Arrange the chopped peaches evenly over the mixture.

*4* For the topping, combine the oats and sugar in a small bowl. Melt the butter, then stir into the bowl to make a crumbly mix. Spread evenly over the peaches.

*5* Bake in the preheated oven for about 1 hour, or until risen, firm, and golden brown. Let cool in the pan for 2–3 minutes, then remove the sides and finish cooling on a wire rack. Best eaten on the day of making.

# peach & cinnamon pie

## ingredients

*serves 6*

oil or melted butter,
   for greasing
1½ cups all-purpose flour
2 tsp baking powder
1 tsp ground cinnamon
¾ cup unsalted butter, softened
¾ cup superfine sugar
3 eggs, beaten
1 tsp vanilla extract
3 ripe peaches or nectarines,
   peeled, pitted, and coarsely
   chopped
2½ cups cornflakes, lightly
   crushed
cream, to serve

## method

1 Preheat the oven to 325°F/160°C. Grease and line the bottom of a 9-inch/23-cm round springform cake pan.

2 Sift the flour, baking powder, and cinnamon into a large bowl and add the butter, sugar, eggs, and vanilla extract. Beat well until the mixture is smooth.

3 Spoon half the mixture into the prepared pan and smooth the surface with a spatula. Arrange the peaches on top. Stir the cornflakes lightly into the remaining mixture and drop spoonfuls of the mix over the peaches.

4 Bake in the preheated oven for about 1 hour, or until risen, firm, and golden brown. Serve hot with cream.

# tropical fruit ring

## ingredients

### serves 12

oil or melted butter,
    for greasing
2 tbsp lime juice
scant 1/2 cup finely chopped dried
    tropical fruit, such as mango,
    papaya and/or pineapple, plus
    extra to decorate
1 1/2 cups all-purpose flour
2 1/2 tsp baking powder
3/4 cup unsalted butter, softened
generous 3/4 cup superfine sugar
3 eggs, beaten
1 tsp vanilla extract

### icing

2/3 cup confectioners' sugar
1 tbsp lime juice

## method

*1* Preheat the oven to 325°F/160°C. Grease a 6 3/4-cup tube cake pan, preferably nonstick. Stir the lime juice into the dried tropical fruit and let soak for 15 minutes.

*2* Sift the flour and baking powder into a large bowl and add the butter, superfine sugar, eggs, and vanilla extract. Beat well until the mixture is smooth, then stir in the soaked fruit.

*3* Spoon the mixture into the prepared pan and level the top with a spatula. Bake in the preheated oven for 40–50 minutes, or until risen, firm, and golden brown. Let cool in the pan for 10 minutes, then turn out and finish cooling on a wire rack.

*4* For the icing, sift the confectioners' sugar into a bowl, add the lime juice, and stir until smooth. Spoon the icing over the cake and decorate with dried tropical fruit. Let set before slicing.

# kiwi fruit cake with lemon frosting

## ingredients

*serves 8*

oil or melted butter,
    for greasing
1½ cups all-purpose flour
2 tsp baking powder
¾ cup unsalted butter, softened
generous ¾ cup superfine sugar
3 eggs, beaten
1 tsp vanilla extract
2 kiwis, peeled and chopped
    into ½-inch/1-cm dice
kiwi slices, to decorate

### frosting

¼ cup cream cheese
1 tbsp grated lemon rind
1 cup confectioners' sugar

## method

*1* Preheat the oven to 325°F/160°C. Grease and line a 5-cup loaf pan.

*2* Sift the flour and baking powder into a large bowl and add the butter, superfine sugar, eggs, and vanilla extract. Beat well until the mixture is smooth. Stir in half the chopped kiwi.

*3* Spoon the mixture into the prepared pan and smooth the surface with a spatula. Sprinkle with the remaining chopped kiwi. Bake in the preheated oven for about 1 hour, or until risen, firm, and golden brown.

*4* Let cool in the pan for 10 minutes, then turn out and finish cooling on a wire rack.

*5* For the frosting, beat together the cream cheese, lemon rind, and confectioners' sugar until smooth. Spread the frosting over the cake and top with kiwi slices.

# citrus mousse cake

## ingredients

*serves 12*

oil or melted butter,
    for greasing
¾ cup butter
¾ cup superfine sugar
4 eggs, lightly beaten
1¾ cups self-rising flour
1 tbsp unsweetened cocoa
1¾ oz/50 g orange-flavored
    semisweet chocolate, melted
peeled orange segments,
    to decorate

### filling & topping

2 eggs, separated
4 tbsp superfine sugar
¾ cup freshly squeezed
    orange juice
2 tsp gelatin
3 tbsp water
1¼ cups heavy cream

## method

*1* Preheat the oven to 350°F/180°C. Grease an 8-inch/
20-cm round springform cake pan and line the bottom
with parchment paper.

*2* Beat the butter and sugar in a bowl until light and
fluffy. Add the eggs, beating in well. Sift together
the flour and cocoa and then fold into the creamed
mixture. Fold in the melted chocolate. Pour into the
prepared pan and smooth level. Bake in the preheated
oven for 40 minutes, or until springy to the touch. Let
cool for 5 minutes in the pan, then turn out onto a wire
rack and let cool completely. Cut into two layers.

*3* For the filling, beat the egg yolks and sugar until pale,
then beat in the orange juice. Sprinkle the gelatin
over the water in a small heatproof bowl and let it go
spongy, then place over a saucepan of hot water and
stir until dissolved. Stir into the egg yolk mixture.

*4* Whip the cream until holding its shape. Reserve a little
for decoration and fold the remainder into the mousse.
Beat the egg whites until standing in soft peaks, then
fold in. Let stand in a cool place until starting to set,
stirring occasionally. Place one half of the cake in
the cake pan. Pour in the mousse and press the second
cake half on top. Chill until set. Transfer to a plate, pipe
cream on the top, and decorate with orange segments.

# lemon cornmeal cake

## ingredients

*serves 8*

scant 1 cup unsalted butter,
    plus extra for greasing
1 cup superfine sugar
finely grated rind and juice of
    1 large lemon
3 eggs, beaten
1¼ cups ground almonds
scant ¾ cup quick-cook
    cornmeal
1 tsp baking powder
sour cream, to serve

### syrup

juice of 2 lemons
¼ cup superfine sugar
2 tbsp water

## method

*1* Preheat the oven to 350°F/180°C. Lightly grease an 8-inch/20-cm round deep cake pan and line the bottom with parchment paper.

*2* Beat together the butter and sugar until pale and fluffy. Beat in the lemon rind, lemon juice, eggs, and ground almonds. Sift in the cornmeal and baking powder and stir until evenly mixed.

*3* Spoon the batter into the prepared pan and spread evenly. Bake in the preheated oven for 30–35 minutes, or until just firm to the touch and golden brown. Remove the cake from the oven and cool in the pan for 20 minutes.

*4* For the syrup, place the lemon juice, sugar, and water in a small saucepan. Heat gently, stirring until the sugar has dissolved, then bring to a boil and simmer for 3–4 minutes, or until slightly reduced and syrupy.

*5* Turn out the cake onto a wire rack, then drizzle half of the syrup evenly over the surface. Let cool completely.

*6* Cut the cake into slices, drizzle the extra syrup over the top, and serve with sour cream.

# orange & poppyseed bundt cake

## ingredients

*serves 10*

scant 1 cup unsalted butter,
   plus extra for greasing
1 cup superfine sugar
3 extra large eggs, beaten
finely grated rind of 1 orange
¼ cup poppy seeds
2¼ cups all-purpose flour,
   plus extra for dusting
2 tsp baking powder
⅔ cup milk
½ cup orange juice
strips of orange zest, to decorate

### syrup

scant ¾ cup superfine sugar
⅔ cup orange juice

## method

*1* Preheat the oven to 325°F/160°C. Grease and lightly flour a Bundt ring pan, about 9½ inches/24 cm in diameter and with a capacity of approximately 8¾ cups.

*2* Cream together the butter and sugar until pale and fluffy, then add the eggs gradually, beating thoroughly after each addition. Stir in the orange rind and poppy seeds. Sift in the flour and baking powder, then fold in evenly.

*3* Add the milk and orange juice, stirring to mix evenly. Spoon the batter into the prepared pan and bake in the preheated oven for 45–50 minutes, or until firm and golden brown. Cool in the pan for 10 minutes, then turn out onto a wire rack to cool.

*4* For the syrup, place the sugar and orange juice in a saucepan and heat gently until the sugar melts. Bring to a boil and simmer for about 5 minutes, until reduced and syrupy.

*5* Spoon the syrup over the cake while it is still warm. Top with the strips of orange zest and serve warm or cold.

# whole orange & almond cake

## ingredients

*serves 8–10*

oil or melted butter,
    for greasing
2 oranges
½ cup ground almonds
1 cup all-purpose flour
1 tbsp baking powder
6 tbsp unsalted butter, softened
generous ¾ cup superfine sugar
3 eggs, beaten
1 tsp orange flower water
2 tbsp orange juice
2 tbsp toasted slivered almonds
strips of orange zest,
    to decorate

## method

*1* Grease and line a 9-inch/23-cm round deep cake pan.

*2* Wash the oranges and put into a pan, then cover with boiling water and simmer, covered, for 1 hour, until soft. Drain and let cool slightly, then cut in half and remove any seeds. Process in a food processor or blender until smooth, then stir in the ground almonds.

*3* Preheat the oven to 325°F/160°C. Sift the flour and baking powder into a large bowl and add the butter, sugar, eggs, and orange flower water. Beat well until the mixture is smooth. Add the orange and almond mixture and the orange juice, mixing evenly.

*4* Spoon the mixture into the prepared pan and smooth the surface with a spatula. Bake in the preheated oven for 40–50 minutes, or until the cake is firm and golden brown.

*5* Let cool in the pan for 2–3 minutes, then turn out and serve warm, topped with slivered almonds and strips of orange zest.

# clementine cake

## ingredients

### serves 8

¾ cup butter, softened,
    plus extra for greasing
2 clementines
¾ cup superfine sugar
3 eggs, lightly beaten
1¼ cups self-rising flour
3 tbsp ground almonds
3 tbsp light cream

### glaze & topping

6 tbsp clementine juice
2 tbsp superfine sugar
3 white sugar lumps, crushed

## method

*1* Preheat the oven to 350°F/180°C. Grease a 7-inch/ 18-cm round cake pan with butter and line the bottom with baking parchment.

*2* Pare the zest from the clementines and chop it finely. In a bowl, cream together the butter, sugar, and clementine zest until pale and fluffy. Gradually add the beaten eggs to the batter, beating thoroughly after each addition.

*3* Gently fold in the flour, ground almonds, and light cream. Spoon the batter into the prepared pan.

*4* Bake in the preheated oven, for 55–60 minutes, or until a fine skewer inserted into the center comes out clean. Let cool slightly.

*5* Meanwhile, make the glaze. Put the clementine juice into a small pan with the superfine sugar. Bring to a boil over a low heat and simmer for 5 minutes.

*6* Turn out the cake onto a wire rack. Drizzle the glaze over the cake until it has been absorbed and sprinkle with the crushed sugar lumps. Let cool completely before serving.

# mango & coconut brûlée cake

## ingredients

**serves 6**

oil or melted butter,
    for greasing
1 large ripe mango, peeled,
    pitted, and diced
1½ cups all-purpose flour
1 tbsp baking powder
¾ cup unsalted butter, softened
generous ¾ cup superfine sugar
3 eggs, beaten
2 tbsp lime juice
finely grated rind of 1 lime
⅓ cup dry unsweetened coconut
2 tbsp granulated sugar
toasted long-shred coconut,
    to decorate

## method

1 Preheat the oven to 350°F/180°C. Grease and line the bottom of a 9-inch/23-cm round deep cake pan.

2 Arrange the mango evenly over the bottom of the pan. Sift the flour and baking powder into a large bowl and add the butter, superfine sugar, and eggs. Beat well until the mixture is smooth, then stir in the lime juice, lime rind, and dry unsweetened coconut.

3 Spoon the mixture over the mango and smooth the surface with a spatula. Bake in the preheated oven for 40–50 minutes, or until risen and golden brown.

4 Let cool in the pan for 2–3 minutes, then invert onto a flameproof dish. Preheat the broiler to high. Sprinkle the top of the cake with the granulated sugar and place under the hot broiler for 2–3 minutes, until browned. Alternatively, use a chef's blowtorch to brown the top.

5 Serve hot, sprinkled with coconut shreds and cut into slices.

# caramel apple upside-down cake

## ingredients

**serves 6**

oil or melted butter,
    for greasing
1½ cups all-purpose flour
1 tbsp baking powder
¾ cup unsalted butter, softened
generous ¾ cup superfine sugar
3 eggs, beaten
1 tsp vanilla extract
finely grated rind of 1 lemon

**topping**

¼ cup unsalted butter
½ cup superfine sugar
1 tbsp water
4 apples
2 tbsp lemon juice

## method

*1* Preheat the oven to 350°F/180°C. Grease a 9-inch/
23-cm round deep cake pan with a solid bottom.

*2* For the caramel apple topping, put the butter and
sugar into a heavy pan with the water and heat gently
until melted, then bring to a boil. Reduce the heat and
cook, stirring, until it turns to a deep golden caramel
color. Pour quickly into the cake pan, tilting to cover
the bottom evenly.

*3* Peel, core, and thickly slice the apples, toss in the
lemon juice, and spread evenly over the bottom of the
cake pan.

*4* Sift the flour and baking powder into a large bowl
and add the butter, sugar, eggs, and vanilla extract.
Beat well until the mixture is smooth, then stir in the
lemon rind.

*5* Spoon the mixture over the apples and smooth the
surface with a spatula. Bake in the preheated oven for
40–50 minutes, or until risen and golden brown.

*6* Let cool in the pan for 2–3 minutes, then turn out
carefully onto a warmed serving plate.

# spiced apple & raisin cake

## ingredients

*serves 8–10*

1 cup unsalted butter, softened, plus extra for greasing
generous 1 cup light brown sugar
4 large eggs, lightly beaten
scant 1²/₃ cups self-rising flour
2 tsp ground cinnamon
½ tsp ground nutmeg
½ cup golden raisins
3 small apples, peeled, cored, and thinly sliced
2 tbsp honey, warmed

## method

*1* Preheat the oven to 350°F/180°C. Grease a 9-inch/23-cm round springform cake pan and line the bottom with parchment paper.

*2* Place the butter and sugar in a large bowl and beat together until light and fluffy. Gradually beat in the eggs. Sift the flour, cinnamon, and nutmeg into the batter and fold in gently using a metal spoon. Fold in the golden raisins.

*3* Spoon half the batter into the prepared pan and level the surface. Scatter over half the sliced apples. Spoon over the rest of the cake mixture and gently level the surface. Arrange the rest of the apple slices over the top.

*4* Bake in the preheated oven for about 1¼ hours until risen, golden brown, and firm to the touch. Let cool in the pan for 10 minutes, then turn out onto a wire rack. Brush the top with the warmed honey and let cool completely.

# prune & armagnac cake

## ingredients

*serves 8*

oil or melted butter,
    for greasing
1⅓ cups plumped dried prunes
⅔ cup apple juice
3 tbsp armagnac or port
1½ cups all-purpose flour
2 tsp baking powder
¾ cup unsalted butter, softened
generous ¾ cup light
    brown sugar
3 eggs, beaten
1 tsp vanilla extract
1 tbsp raw brown sugar
cream or yogurt, to serve

## method

1 Preheat the oven to 325°F/160°C. Grease and line a 9-inch/23-cm round cake pan.

2 Put the prunes into a pan with the apple juice and bring to a boil. Reduce the heat and simmer gently for 10 minutes, until the liquid is absorbed. Spoon the armagnac over them and let cool completely.

3 Sift the flour and baking powder into a large bowl and add the butter, light brown sugar, eggs, and vanilla extract. Beat well until the mixture is smooth.

4 Spoon the mixture into the prepared pan and smooth the surface with a spatula. Drain the prunes well, reserving the juices, and arrange the prunes over the mixture in a single layer.

5 Bake in the preheated oven for 40–50 minutes, or until risen, firm, and golden brown. Turn out onto a warmed serving plate with the prunes at the bottom and spoon the reserved juices over the cake. Sprinkle with the raw brown sugar and serve in slices, with cream or yogurt.

# glazed fruit & nut cake

## ingredients

*serves 16–18*

oil or melted butter,
   for greasing
2¼ cups all-purpose flour,
   plus extra for dusting
1 tbsp baking powder
1 tsp apple pie spice
¾ cup unsalted butter,
   softened
generous ¾ cup dark
   brown sugar
3 eggs, beaten
1 tsp vanilla extract
2 tbsp milk
2 cups mixed dried fruit
¾ cup chopped mixed nuts

### topping

3 tbsp honey, warmed
1½ cups mixed candied fruits,
   such as pineapple,
   cherries, and orange
½ cup whole shelled nuts,
   such as Brazil nuts,
   almonds, and walnuts

## method

1 Preheat the oven to 325°F/160°C. Grease a 9-inch/
   23-cm round springform cake pan and dust lightly
   with flour.

2 Sift the flour, baking powder, and apple pie spice into a
   large bowl and add the butter, sugar, eggs, and vanilla
   extract. Beat well until the mixture is smooth, then stir
   in the milk, mixed dried fruit, and chopped nuts.

3 Spoon the batter into the prepared pan and smooth
   level. Bake in the preheated oven for about 1 hour, or
   until risen, firm, and golden brown.

4 Let cool in the pan for 30 minutes, then remove the
   sides and place on a wire rack to finish cooling.

5 Brush the top of the cake with a little of the warmed
   honey, then arrange the candied fruits and whole nuts
   on top. Brush with the remaining honey and let set.

# summer berry macaroons

## ingredients

**makes 6**

¾ cup ground almonds
1 cup confectioners' sugar
2 extra large egg whites
¼ cup superfine sugar
fresh mint sprigs and whole
     strawberries, to decorate

### filling

⅔ cup heavy cream
2 tbsp lemon curd
generous ¾ cup hulled and sliced
     strawberries, plus extra whole
     strawberries to decorate
generous ¾ cup raspberries
2 tbsp confectioners' sugar

## method

**1** Place the ground almonds and confectioners' sugar in a food processor and process for 15 seconds. Sift the mixture into a bowl. Line 2 baking sheets with parchment paper.

**2** Place the egg whites in a large bowl and whip until holding soft peaks. Gradually beat in the superfine sugar to make a firm, glossy meringue. Using a spatula, fold the almond mixture into the meringue one-third at a time. When all the dry ingredients are thoroughly incorporated, continue to cut and fold the mixture until it forms a shiny batter with a thick consistency.

**3** Pour the batter into a pastry bag fitted with a ½-inch/1-cm plain tip. Pipe 12 large circles onto the prepared baking sheets. Let stand at room temperature for 30 minutes. Preheat the oven to 325°F/160°C and bake for 15–20 minutes. Cool for 10 minutes, peel off the parchment paper and let cool.

**4** For the filling, whip the cream until holding soft peaks, then fold in the lemon curd. Top half the macaroon shells with the lemon cream and arrange two-thirds of the berries. Puree the remaining berries with the confectioners' sugar. Drizzle a little of the puree over the berries and top with the remaining macaroons. Serve decorated with mint sprigs and strawberries.

# blueberry cheesecake macaroons

## ingredients

**makes 16**

¾ cup ground almonds
1 cup confectioners' sugar
2 extra large egg whites
¼ cup superfine sugar
½ tsp vanilla extract
blue food coloring paste
    or liquid

### filling

½ cup cream cheese
2 tbsp sour cream
1 tbsp confectioners' sugar
generous ½ cup blueberries

## method

*1* Place the ground almonds and confectioners' sugar in a food processor and process for 15 seconds. Sift into a bowl. Line 2 baking sheets with parchment paper.

*2* Place the egg whites in a large bowl and whip until holding soft peaks. Gradually beat in the superfine sugar to make a firm, glossy meringue. Beat in the vanilla extract and blue food coloring.

*3* Using a spatula, fold the almond mixture into the meringue one-third at a time. When all the dry ingredients are thoroughly incorporated, continue to cut and fold the mixture until it forms a shiny batter with a thick, ribbonlike consistency.

*4* Pour the batter into a pastry bag fitted with a ½-inch/1-cm plain tip. Pipe 32 small circles onto the prepared baking sheets. Let stand at room temperature for 30 minutes. Preheat the oven to 325°F/160°C.

*5* Bake in the preheated oven for 10–15 minutes. Cool for 10 minutes. Carefully peel the macaroons off the parchment paper and let cool completely.

*6* For the filling, beat the cream cheese, sour cream, and confectioners' sugar together until smooth. Lightly crush the blueberries and fold into the cream cheese mixture. Use to sandwich pairs of macaroons together.

# celebration cakes

# birthday number cake

## ingredients

*serves 10–12*

oil or melted butter,
    for greasing
1½ cups all-purpose flour
1 tbsp baking powder
¾ cup unsalted butter,
    softened
generous ¾ cup superfine sugar
3 eggs, beaten
1 tsp vanilla extract
2 tbsp orange juice
finely grated rind of ½ orange
sugar orange slices and birthday
    candles, to decorate

### frosting

3 cups confectioners' sugar, sifted
¾ cup unsalted butter, softened
finely grated rind of ½ orange
1 tbsp orange juice

## method

*1* Preheat the oven to 325°F/160°C. Grease and line a
    10- x 7-inch/25- x 18-cm numeral cake pan or a frame
    on a cookie sheet, about 2 inches/5 cm deep.

*2* Sift the flour and baking powder into a large bowl
    and add the butter, superfine sugar, eggs, and vanilla
    extract. Beat well until the mixture is smooth, then stir
    in the orange juice and rind.

*3* Spoon the mixture into the prepared pan and smooth
    the surface with a spatula. Bake in the preheated
    oven for 40–50 minutes, or until risen, firm, and golden
    brown. Let cool in the pan for 5 minutes, then turn
    out and finish cooling on a wire rack.

*4* For the frosting, beat together the confectioners'
    sugar, butter, orange rind, and juice until smooth.
    Spread over the cake evenly, smoothing with a spatula.

*5* Arrange the orange slices on top of the cake to
    decorate, then add the birthday candles and serve.

# polka dot birthday cake

## ingredients

*serves 8–10*

oil or melted butter,
　　for greasing
1½ cups all-purpose flour
1 tbsp baking powder
¾ cup unsalted butter, softened
generous ¾ cup superfine sugar
3 eggs, beaten
1 tsp vanilla extract
2 tbsp milk
sugar-coated chocolate candies
　　and birthday candles,
　　to decorate

### filling & topping

5 tbsp apricot jelly
1 tbsp lemon juice
1 lb 2 oz/500 g ready-to-roll
　　fondant

## method

*1* Preheat the oven to 325°F/160°C. Grease and line two 8-inch/20 cm square layer cake pans.

*2* Sift the flour and baking powder into a large bowl and add the butter, sugar, eggs, and vanilla extract. Beat well until the mixture is smooth, then stir in the milk.

*3* Divide the mixture between the prepared pans and smooth the surfaces with a spatula. Bake in the preheated oven for 25–30 minutes, or until risen, firm, and golden brown. Let cool in the pans for 2–3 minutes, then turn out and finish cooling on a wire rack.

*4* Warm the apricot jelly with the lemon juice in a small pan until melted. Spread half over one cake and place the other cake on top. Brush the remaining jelly over the top and sides of the cake.

*5* Roll out the fondant and cover the cakes, smoothing with your hands, then trim the edges with a sharp knife. Decorate with candies and birthday candles.

# mini cake pops

## ingredients

*makes 24*

1 lb/450 g store-bought yellow
   or almond cake
3 oz/85 g mascarpone cheese
generous 1/2 cup confectioners'
   sugar
1/2 tsp vanilla or almond extract

### to decorate

8 oz/225 g milk chocolate,
   coarsely chopped
24 lollipop sticks
scant 1 1/4 cups confectioners'
   sugar
pink food coloring
4 tsp cold water
24 small candies, such as
   miniature sugar-coated
   chocolate candies
sugar sprinkles

## method

*1* Line a baking sheet with parchment paper. Crumble the yellow cake into a mixing bowl. Add the mascarpone, confectioners' sugar, and vanilla and mix together until you have a thick paste.

*2* Divide the paste into 24 even pieces. Roll one piece of the paste into a ball. Push this ball into a mini paper liner, pressing it down so that when it is removed from the liner you have a mini cupcake shape. Shape the remaining 23 cake pops in the same way. Place on the baking sheet and chill for 1–2 hours to firm up.

*3* Put the chocolate in a heatproof bowl, set the bowl over a saucepan of gently simmering water, and heat until melted. Remove from the heat. Push a lollipop stick into each cake pop. Dip a cake pop into the chocolate, turn until coated, letting the excess drip into the bowl. Repeat with the remaining cake pops. Let stand in a cool place until the chocolate has set.

*4* Put the confectioners' sugar in a mixing bowl and beat in a dash of pink food coloring and the water until smooth. The icing should almost hold its shape. Spoon a little onto a cake pop, easing it slightly down the sides with the side of a teaspoon. Before the icing sets, place a small candy in the center of each cake pop and scatter with sugar sprinkles.

# tutti frutti whoopie pies

## ingredients

*makes 25*

generous 1¾ cups all-purpose
    flour
1 tsp baking soda
large pinch of salt
½ cup butter, softened
¾ cup superfine sugar
1 large egg, beaten
½ tsp vanilla extract
⅔ cup buttermilk
½ cup finely chopped mixed
    colored candied cherries
4 tbsp multicolored sugar
    sprinkles

### filling

8oz/225 g white marshmallows
4 tbsp milk
few drops of red food coloring
½ cup vegetable shortening
½ cup confectioners' sugar, sifted

## method

*1* Preheat the oven to 350°F/180°C. Line 2–3 large
    cookie sheets with parchment paper. Sift together the
    all-purpose flour, baking soda, and salt. Place the butter
    and sugar in a large bowl and beat with an electric
    mixer until pale and fluffy. Beat in the egg and vanilla
    extract followed by half of the flour mixture and then
    the buttermilk. Stir in the rest of the flour mixture and
    mix until incorporated. Stir in the chopped cherries.

*2* Pipe or spoon 50 small mounds of the batter onto the
    prepared cookie sheets, spaced well apart to allow for
    spreading. Bake in the preheated oven, one sheet at a
    time, for 9–11 minutes, until risen and just firm to the
    touch. Cool for 5 minutes, then using a palette knife
    transfer to a cooling rack and let cool completely.

*3* For the filling, place the marshmallows, milk, and food
    coloring in a heatproof bowl set over a pan of water.
    Heat until the marshmallows have melted. Remove
    from the heat and let cool.

*4* Place the vegetable shortening and confectioners'
    sugar in a bowl and beat together until smooth and
    creamy. Add the creamed mixture to the marshmallow
    and beat for 1–2 minutes until fluffy. Spread the filling
    over the flat side of half the cakes. Top with the remaining
    cakes. Roll the edges of the pies in the sugar sprinkles.

# violet & lavender macaroons

## ingredients

*makes 16*

¾ cup ground almonds
1 cup confectioners' sugar
2 extra large egg whites
¼ cup lavender sugar
violet food coloring paste or liquid
1 tsp candied violets
1 tsp dried lavender

### filling

½ cup cream cheese
2 tbsp lavender sugar

## method

**1** Place the ground almonds and confectioners' sugar in a food processor and process for 15 seconds. Sift into a bowl. Line 2 baking sheets with parchment paper.

**2** Place the egg whites in a large bowl and whip until holding soft peaks. Gradually beat in the lavender sugar to make a firm, glossy meringue. Beat in enough food coloring to give a pale violet color.

**3** Using a spatula, fold the almond mixture into the meringue one-third at a time. When all the dry ingredients are thoroughly incorporated, continue to cut and fold the mixture until it forms a shiny batter with a thick consistency. Pour the batter into a pastry bag fitted with a ½-inch/1-cm plain tip. Pipe 32 small circles onto the prepared baking sheets. Tap the baking sheets firmly onto a work surface to remove air bubbles. Sprinkle over the candied violets and dried lavender. Let stand at room temperature for 30 minutes. Preheat the oven to 325°F/160°C.

**4** Bake in the preheated oven for 10–15 minutes. Cool for 10 minutes. Carefully peel the macaroons off the parchment paper and let cool completely.

**5** For the filling, beat together the cream cheese and lavender sugar until smooth. Use to sandwich pairs of macaroons together.

# white chocolate valentine's gâteau

## ingredients

*serves 10*

oil or melted butter,
    for greasing
1½ cups all-purpose flour
1 tbsp baking powder
¾ cup unsalted butter,
    softened
generous ¾ cup superfine sugar
3 eggs, beaten
1 tsp vanilla extract
¼ cup grated white chocolate
2 tbsp white rum (optional)
candied violets, to decorate

### frosting

7 oz/200 g white chocolate,
    broken into pieces
2 tbsp milk
scant 1 cup heavy cream

## method

*1* Preheat the oven to 325°F/160°C. Grease a 6¾-cup heart-shape cake pan.

*2* Sift the flour and baking powder into a bowl and add the butter, sugar, eggs, and vanilla extract. Beat well until smooth, then stir in the grated chocolate.

*3* Spoon the mixture into the prepared pan and spread the top level. Bake in the preheated oven for 45–55 minutes, or until risen, firm, and golden brown. Let cool in the pan for 10 minutes, then turn out onto a wire rack to finish cooling.

*4* For the frosting, melt the chocolate with the milk in a heatproof bowl set over a pan of hot water. Remove from the heat and stir until smooth, then let cool for 10 minutes. Whip the cream until it holds soft peaks, then fold into the cooled chocolate mixture.

*5* Sprinkle the cake with the rum, if using. Spread the frosting over the top and sides of the cake, swirling with a spatula, then decorate with candied violets.

# valentine chocolate heart cake

## ingredients

*serves 12*

1½ cups self-rising flour
2 tsp baking powder
½ cup unsweetened cocoa
3 eggs
scant ¾ cup light brown sugar
⅔ cup sunflower oil,
    plus extra for greasing
⅔ cup light cream
fresh mint sprigs, to decorate

### filling & topping

8 oz/225 g semisweet chocolate,
    broken into pieces
generous 1 cup heavy cream
3 tbsp seedless raspberry jelly
generous 1 cup fresh or
    frozen raspberries

## method

*1* Preheat the oven to 350°F/180°C. Grease an 8 inch/ 20 cm wide heart-shape cake pan and line the bottom with parchment paper.

*2* Sift the flour, baking powder, and cocoa into a large bowl. Beat the eggs with the sugar, oil, and light cream. Make a well in the dry ingredients and add the egg mixture, then stir to mix thoroughly, beating to a smooth batter.

*3* Pour the batter into the prepared pan and bake in the preheated oven for 25–30 minutes, or until risen and firm to the touch. Cool in the pan for 10 minutes, then turn out and finish cooling on a wire rack.

*4* For the filling and topping, place the chocolate and heavy cream in a saucepan over low heat and stir until melted. Remove from the heat and stir until the mixture cools slightly and begins to thicken.

*5* Use a sharp knife to cut the cake in half horizontally. Spread the cut surface of each half with the raspberry jelly, then top with about 3 tablespoons of the chocolate mixture. Sprinkle over half the raspberries and replace the top, pressing down lightly. Spread the remaining chocolate mixture over the top and sides of the cake, swirling with a spatula. Top with the remaining raspberries and decorate with mint sprigs.

# easter marzipan fruitcake

## ingredients

*serves 16*

³⁄₄ cup unsalted butter,
    plus extra for greasing
scant 1 cup light brown sugar
3 eggs, beaten
2 cups all-purpose flour
¹⁄₂ tsp baking powder
2 tsp apple pie spice
finely grated rind of 1 small lemon
scant ¹⁄₂ cup currants
scant ³⁄₄ cup golden raisins
¹⁄₃ cup chopped candied peel
1 lb 9 oz/700 g marzipan
3 tbsp apricot jelly

## method

1 Preheat the oven to 300°F/150°C. Grease and line an 8-inch/20-cm round deep cake pan with parchment paper.

2 Place the butter and sugar in a bowl and cream together with an electric whisk until pale, light, and fluffy. Gradually beat in the eggs. Sift together the flour, baking powder, and apple pie spice. Use a large metal spoon to fold into the creamed mixture. Stir in the lemon rind, currants, golden raisins, and candied peel, mixing evenly. Spoon half the batter into the prepared pan and smooth level.

3 Roll out 9 oz/250 g of the marzipan to an 8-inch/20-cm round and place over the batter in the pan. Add the remaining cake batter and smooth level. Bake the cake in the preheated oven for 2¹⁄₄–2³⁄₄ hours, or until firm and golden and the sides are beginning to shrink away from the pan. Let cool in the pan for 30 minutes, then turn out onto a wire rack to finish cooling.

4 Brush the top of the cake with apricot jelly. Roll out two thirds of the remaining marzipan to a round to cover the top of the cake. Use a knife to mark a lattice design in the surface and pinch the edges to decorate. Roll the remaining marzipan into eleven small balls and arrange around the cake. Place under a hot broiler for 30–40 seconds to brown lightly. Cool before storing.

# easter cupcakes

## ingredients

### makes 12

½ cup butter, softened or soft
    margarine
generous ½ cup superfine sugar
2 eggs, lightly beaten
⅔ cup self-rising flour
¼ cup unsweetened cocoa
9 oz/250 g mini sugar-coated
    chocolate eggs, to decorate

### frosting

6 tbsp butter, softened
1 cup confectioners' sugar
1 tbsp milk
2–3 drops vanilla extract

## method

*1* Preheat the oven to 350°F/180°C. Line a 12-hole muffin pan with 12 paper liners or put 12 double-layer paper liners on a baking sheet.

*2* Place the butter and sugar in a large bowl and beat together until light and fluffy, then gradually beat in the eggs. Sift in the flour and cocoa and fold into the batter. Spoon the batter into the paper liners.

*3* Bake in the preheated oven for 15–20 minutes, or until well risen and springy to the touch. Transfer to a wire rack to cool completely.

*4* For the frosting, place the butter in a bowl. Sift in the confectioners' sugar and beat together until well mixed, adding the milk and vanilla extract.

*5* When the cupcakes are cold, place the frosting in a pastry bag fitted with a large star tip, and pipe a circle around the edge of each cupcake to form a nest. Place chocolate eggs in the center of each nest to decorate.

# silver wedding anniversary cake

## ingredients

*serves 10–12*

oil or melted butter,
    for greasing
1½ cups all-purpose flour
1 tbsp baking powder
¾ cup unsalted butter,
    softened
generous ¾ cup superfine sugar
3 eggs, beaten
1 tsp vanilla extract
2 tbsp milk
2 tbsp medium sherry
silver balls, to decorate

### frosting

generous 1 cup mascarpone
    cheese
3 tbsp light cream
2¼ cups confectioners' sugar,
    sifted, plus extra if needed

## method

*1* Preheat the oven to 350°F/180°C. Grease and line the bottoms of a 7-inch/18-cm layer cake pan and a 9-inch/23-cm layer cake pan.

*2* Sift the flour and baking powder into a large bowl and add the butter, superfine sugar, eggs, and vanilla extract. Beat well until the mixture is smooth, then stir in the milk.

*3* Spoon the mixture into the prepared pans and smooth the surfaces with a spatula. Bake in the preheated oven for 20–25 minutes for the small cake and 25–30 minutes for the large cake, or until risen, firm, and golden brown.

*4* Cool the cakes in the pans for 2–3 minutes, then turn out and finish cooling on wire racks. Prick the cakes with a skewer and sprinkle with sherry.

*5* For the frosting, beat together the mascarpone, cream, and confectioners' sugar to a smooth, spreading consistency, adding a little more confectioners' sugar if needed. Spread a little frosting on top of the center of the larger cake, then place the small cake on top, pressing down lightly.

*6* Spread the remaining frosting over the cakes, swirling with a spatula. Decorate with silver balls before serving

# rose gâteau

## ingredients

*serves 8–10*

oil or melted butter,
    for greasing
1½ cups all-purpose flour
1 tbsp baking powder
¾ cup unsalted butter, softened
generous ¾ cup superfine sugar
3 eggs, beaten
1 tsp rose water
2 tbsp milk

**filling & icing**
⅔ cup heavy cream
1 tsp rose water
1¾ cups confectioners' sugar,
    sifted

**to decorate**
fresh rose petals, washed and
    patted dry
½ egg white
superfine sugar, for sprinkling

## method

**1** Preheat the oven to 350°F/180°C. Grease and line the bottoms of two 9-inch/23-cm layer cake pans.

**2** Sift the flour and baking powder into a large bowl and add the butter, superfine sugar, eggs, and rose water. Beat well until the mixture is smooth, then stir in the milk.

**3** Divide the mixture between the prepared pans and smooth the surfaces with a spatula. Bake in the preheated oven for 25–30 minutes, or until risen, firm, and golden brown. Let cool in the pans for 2–3 minutes, then turn out and finish cooling on a wire rack.

**4** For the filling, whip the cream with ½ teaspoon of the rose water until just thick enough to hold its shape. Use to sandwich the cakes together.

**5** For the icing, combine the confectioners' sugar with the remaining rose water and just enough water to mix to a thick pouring consistency. Spoon it over the cake, letting it drizzle down the sides. Let set.

**6** Brush the rose petals with the egg white, sprinkle with superfine sugar, and arrange on top of the cake, to decorate.

# halloween pumpkin cake

## ingredients

*serves 10*

oil or melted butter,
    for greasing
1½ cups all-purpose flour
1 tbsp baking powder
1 tsp pumpkin pie spice
¾ cup unsalted butter,
    softened
generous ¾ cup light
    brown sugar
3 eggs, beaten
1 tsp vanilla extract
1½ cups coarsely grated
    pumpkin flesh

### topping

3 tbsp apricot jelly, warmed
a few drops of orange and black
    food colorings
1 lb 12 oz/800 g ready-to-roll
    fondant
black, green, and yellow
    writing icing

## method

1 Preheat the oven to 325°F/160°C. Grease and line a 9-inch/23-cm round, deep cake pan.

2 Sift the flour, baking powder, and pumpkin pie spice into a bowl and add the butter, sugar, eggs, and vanilla extract. Beat well until smooth, then stir in the pumpkin.

3 Spoon the mixture into the prepared pan and spread the top level. Bake in the preheated oven for 40–50 minutes, or until well risen, firm, and golden brown. Let cool in the pan for 10 minutes, then turn out onto a wire rack to finish cooling.

4 Brush the cake with the warmed apricot jelly. Knead orange food coloring into about three-quarters of the fondant and roll out to cover the top and sides of the cake. Trim the edges neatly, reserving the trimmings.

5 Form the trimmings into small pumpkin shapes, then use the black writing icing to pipe faces and the green writing icing to pipe stalks onto them. Knead black food coloring into the remaining fondant, then roll it out and cut into bat shapes. Pipe eyes onto the bats using yellow writing icing, then place the pumpkins and bats onto the cake to decorate.

# halloween spider's web cake

## ingredients

### serves 8–10

½ cup unsalted butter,
  plus extra for greasing
generous ½ cup superfine sugar
2 eggs, beaten
3 tbsp milk
1¼ cups self-rising flour
½ tsp baking powder
a few drops of orange food
  coloring

### topping

2 tbsp apricot jelly, warmed
1 lb 2 oz/500 g ready-to-roll
  fondant (three-quarters
  colored orange and one
  quarter black)
scant 1 cup confectioners' sugar,
  plus extra for dusting

## method

**1** Preheat the oven to 325°F/160°C. Grease an 18-cm/7-inch round cake pan and line the base with parchment paper.

**2** Cream together the butter and superfine sugar until light and fluffy. Beat in the eggs and milk. Sift in the flour and baking powder, then fold in. Spoon half the mixture into a separate bowl and stir in a few drops of orange food coloring. Place alternate spoonfuls of the plain and orange batters into the prepared cake pan, swirling lightly for a marbled effect. Bake in the preheated oven for 35–40 minutes. Leave to cool, then turn out and finish cooling on a wire rack.

**3** Place the cake on a plate and brush the top and sides with apricot jelly. Roll out the orange fondant on a counter lightly dusted with confectioners' sugar, then lift it onto the cake. Trim, reserving the trimmings.

**4** Place the confectioners' sugar in a bowl and stir in enough water to mix to a paste, adding a few drops of black food coloring. Spoon into a small pastry bag with a medium plain tip, then pipe a spider's web design over the top of the cake. Shape about half of the black fondant into an oval for the spider's body, then shape eight legs from the black fondant. Shape two eyes from the orange icing fondant. Place on the web.

# pina colada whoopie pies

## ingredients

*makes 12*

generous 1½ cups
    all-purpose flour
2 tsp baking powder
large pinch of salt
⅔ cup dry unsweetened coconut
½ cup butter, softened
¾ cup superfine sugar
1 large egg, beaten
generous ⅓ cup milk
2 tbsp finely chopped
    candied pineapple
toasted unsweetened coconut
    flakes, to decorate

### filling

1¾ cups heavy cream
2 tbsp white rum

### icing

1 cup confectioners' sugar
1–2 tbsp pineapple juice

## method

1 Preheat the oven to 350°F/180°C. Line 2–3 large
   cookie sheets with parchment paper. Sift together
   the all-purpose flour, baking powder, and salt. Stir in
   the coconut.

2 Place the butter and sugar in a large bowl and beat
   with an electric mixer until pale and fluffy. Beat in the
   egg followed by half of the flour mixture and then
   the milk. Stir in the rest of the flour mixture and mix
   until incorporated. Fold in the chopped pineapple.

3 Pipe or spoon 24 mounds of the batter onto the
   prepared cookie sheets, spaced well apart to allow for
   spreading. Bake in the preheated oven, one sheet at a
   time, for 10–12 minutes until risen and just firm to the
   touch. Cool for 5 minutes, then using a palette knife
   transfer to a wire rack and let cool completely.

4 For the filling, place the cream and rum in a bowl and
   whip together until holding firm peaks. For the icing,
   sift the confectioners' sugar into a bowl and gradually
   stir in enough pineapple juice to make a smooth icing.

5 To assemble, spread or pipe the rum cream on the flat
   side of half the cakes. Top with the rest of the cakes.
   Spoon the icing over the whoopie pies letting it drip
   down the sides. Decorate with toasted coconut. Let set.

# christmas macaroons

## ingredients

### makes 16

³/₄ cup ground almonds
1 cup confectioners' sugar
1 tsp ground allspice
2 extra large egg whites
¼ cup superfine sugar
½ tsp freshly grated nutmeg
1 tsp gold dragées

### filling

4 tbsp unsalted butter, softened
finely grated zest and juice of
    ½ orange
1 tsp ground allspice
1 cup confectioners' sugar, sifted
2 tbsp finely chopped candied
    cherries

## method

**1** Place the ground almonds, confectioners' sugar, and allspice in a food processor and process for 15 seconds. Sift the mixture into a bowl. Line 2 baking sheets with parchment paper.

**2** Place the egg whites in a large bowl and whip until holding soft peaks. Gradually beat in the superfine sugar to make a firm, glossy meringue. Using a spatula, fold the almond mixture into the meringue one-third at a time. When all the dry ingredients are thoroughly incorporated, continue to cut and fold the mixture until it forms a shiny batter with a thick consistency.

**3** Pour the batter into a pastry bag fitted with a ½-inch/ 1-cm plain tip. Pipe 32 small circles onto the prepared baking sheets. Sprinkle half the macaroons with the grated nutmeg and the gold dragées. Let stand for 30 minutes. Preheat the oven to 325°F/160°C. Bake in the preheated oven for 10–15 minutes. Cool for 10 minutes then peel the macaroons off the parchment paper and let cool completely.

**4** For the filling, beat the butter and orange juice and zest in a bowl until fluffy. Gradually beat in the allspice and confectioners' sugar until smooth and creamy. Fold in the candied cherries. Use to sandwich pairs of macaroons together.

# golden christmas cake

## ingredients

*serves 16–18*

¾ cup chopped dried apricots
⅓ cup chopped dried mango
⅓ cup chopped
    dried pineapple
generous 1 cup golden raisins
¼ cup chopped
    preserved ginger
⅓ cup chopped candied peel
finely grated zest and juice of
    1 orange
4 tbsp brandy
¾ cup unsalted butter, plus
    extra for greasing
½ cup light brown sugar
4 eggs, beaten
2 tbsp honey
1½ cups self-rising flour
2 tsp ground allspice
¾ cup pecans

### topping
1 lb 12 oz/800 g marzipan
2 lb/900 g ready-to-use
    rolled fondant
silver dragées

## method

*1* Place the chopped apricots, mango, and pineapple in a bowl with the golden raisins, preserved ginger, and candied peel. Stir in the orange zest, orange juice, and brandy. Cover the bowl and let soak overnight.

*2* Preheat the oven to 325°F/160°C. Grease a 9-inch/23-cm round springform cake pan and line with parchment paper.

*3* Cream together the butter and brown sugar until the mixture is pale and fluffy. Add the eggs, beating well between each addition. Stir in the honey. Sift the flour with the allspice and fold into the mixture using a metal spoon. Add the soaked fruit and pecans, stirring thoroughly to mix. Spoon the batter into the prepared pan, spreading it evenly, then make a slight dip in the center.

*4* Place the pan in the center of the preheated oven and bake for 1½–2 hours, or until golden brown and firm to the touch and a toothpick inserted into the center comes out clean. Let cool in the pan.

*5* Turn the cake out, remove the lining paper, and rewrap in clean parchment paper and foil. Store in a cool place for at least 1 month before use. If you want, cover the cake with marzipan and fondant, following the package instructions, and decorate with silver dragées.

# christmas mulled sponge loaf

## ingredients

### serves 8

oil or melted butter,
   for greasing
1½ cups all-purpose flour
1 tbsp baking powder
1 tsp apple pie spice
¾ cup unsalted butter,
   softened
generous ¾ cup light
   brown sugar
3 eggs, beaten
1 tsp vanilla extract
finely grated rind of 1 orange
2 tbsp orange juice

### syrup

⅔ cup confectioners' sugar
scant ½ cup port or red wine
1 piece of star anise

### to decorate

10 fresh cranberries
10 fresh bay leaves
1 egg white
3 tbsp superfine sugar

## method

1 Preheat the oven to 350°F/180°C. Grease a 5-cup loaf pan and line with parchment paper.

2 Sift the flour, baking powder, and apple pie spice into a large bowl and add the butter, brown sugar, eggs, and vanilla extract. Beat well until the mixture is smooth, then stir in the orange rind and juice.

3 Spoon the batter into the prepared pan and smooth level. Bake in the preheated oven for 40–50 minutes, or until risen, firm, and golden brown. (Don't worry if the cake dips slightly in the center.)

4 Remove the pan from the oven and stand it on a wire rack. For the syrup, put the confectioners' sugar, port, and star anise into a pan and heat gently until boiling. Boil rapidly for 2–3 minutes to reduce slightly. Remove the star anise.

5 Spoon the syrup over the top of the cake and let soak for 30 minutes. Turn out the cake from the pan, so it is upside down.

6 Brush the cranberries and bay leaves with the egg white and sprinkle with the superfine sugar, then arrange on top of the cake.

# snowflake whoopie pies

## ingredients

### makes 14

scant 1½ cups all-purpose flour
2 tsp baking powder
large pinch of salt
½ cup ground almonds
½ cup butter, softened
¾ cup superfine sugar,
    plus extra for sprinkling
1 large egg, beaten
1 tsp almond extract
scant ½ cup milk
1 tbsp silver balls

### filling

6 tbsp unsalted butter, softened
½ cup heavy cream
2½ cups confectioners' sugar,
    sifted

### icing

1 cup confectioners' sugar
1–2 tbsp warm water

## method

1 Preheat the oven to 350°F/180°C. Line 2–3 large cookie sheets with parchment paper. Sift together the all-purpose flour, baking powder, and salt. Stir in the ground almonds. Place the butter and sugar in a large bowl and beat with an electric mixer until pale and fluffy. Beat in the egg and almond extract followed by half of the flour mixture and then the milk. Stir in the rest of the flour mixture and beat until incorporated.

2 Pipe or spoon 28 mounds of the batter onto the prepared cookie sheets, spaced well apart to allow for spreading. Bake in the preheated oven, one sheet at a time, for 10–12 minutes until risen and just firm to the touch. Cool for 5 minutes, then using a palette knife transfer to a cooling rack and let cool completely.

3 For the filling, place the butter in a bowl and beat with an electric mixer for 2–3 minutes until pale and creamy. Beat in the cream, then beat in the confectioners' sugar until the buttercream is very light and fluffy. For the icing, sift the confectioners' sugar into a bowl and gradually stir in enough water to make a smooth, thick icing. To assemble, pipe or spread the buttercream on the flat side of half of the cakes. Top with the rest of the cakes. Spoon the icing into a small pastry bag and pipe snowflake patterns on the top. Decorate with silver balls and sprinkle with superfine sugar. Let set.

# index